Steven Ashe was born in 1960, lives in Glastonbury, England and has been actively involved in the literary and practical Qabalah since 1979. and has an B.A. (Hons) Degree in Interactive Multimedia Communication. In addition to his list of published works, including articles for Prediction Magazine, Pan Sothis, Thelemic Magic (Volumes 1 & 2): *Mandrake of Oxford 1994, 1995*, he has produced a series of Audio CDs upon the modus operandi of the Hermetic Qabalah.

His acclaimed published works include Glastonbury Books editions of the monumental ***Complete Golden Dawn Initiate***, ***The Qabalah Codex***, ***The Testament of Solomon*** ISBN: 978-1-4116-6164-6, ***Keys to the Rosicrucian Qabalah*** and the audio CDs ***The Hermetic Qabalah*** and ***The Qabalah: The Book of Calls*** from the same publisher.

His first published full length work upon advanced Qabalistic lore '***Qabalah of 50 Gates***' (*Mandrake of Oxford* ***2002*** / *Glastonbury Books* ***2006***) is considered to be one of the most exciting experimental works of Qabalistic philosophy in the English language.

Glastonbury Books Edition

ISBN: 978-0-9556932-2-9

First Edition

www.glastonburybooks.com

The Testament of Solomon

&

The Wisdom of Solomon

Edited by Steven Ashe

Glastonbury Books 2008

For Kestrel, Alex, Rowan, Natalie & Siara

I would like to acknowledge the friendship and good will of the following, in their assistance and companionship upon the path and advice: Christopher Hyatt, Emma Nicol, David and Patricia Ashe, Stephen Harrington, Jamuna (Bardic Groove), Norma Dellavolta, Steve Davies, Paul Bolton, Michael & Pauline Bottomley, Clive Harper, Brian Radley, Marie Clewley-Radley, Joanne Latham, Ludovic Delaloye, Liz Harnett, Julie Pinner, Julian Caruso, Donna Wright, Laura Woodward, Stuart Atkins, Darcy Kuntz & the GD, Jeanne Wheeler, Diane Edwards, Frances Taylor, Jonathon Edisbury, Joan Corbett, Mark Ferguson, Shirley McIver, Alex Bennett, Robert & Patricia Turner, Jeff Roberts, Sue Render & David Walker of Labyrinth Books (Glastonbury), 'Debs' of The Goddess & the Green Man (Glastonbury), Adrian Ward, Clare Turner, Martin Elmore, Karen Woodhead, & Steve Roberts, Gavin, Bill and Tasha of Courtyard Books Glastonbury.

Foreword

by

Steven Ashe

The oldest surviving copies of *The Testament of Solomon* were written in the same grammatic form as New Testament Greek and have been dated by scholars as originating from the period of the first to fourth centuries (C.E.). Ascribed to the authorship of the Old Testament King Solomon of the *Book of Kings* the work describes how Solomon is enabled to build the Temple by commanding demons by means of a magical ring and its five pointed seal entrusted to him by the Archangel Michael.

Solomon states that he wrote his testament before his death so that the children of Israel would know the powers and shapes of the demons, and the names of the angels who have power over them.

The work details the names of the demons of the 36 *Decans*, divisions of ten degrees, of the three hundred and sixty degree circle of the zodiacal band which appear to be distortions of the traditional names of these D*ecans*. The Testament gives an account of how these demons can be banished, providing instruction regarding the nature and appearance of these entities; for instance, one in the shape of a dog and another who has no head and sees through its breasts, anticipating the *sigils* (signatures) and descriptive pictorial *pseudographia* of later medieval grimoires (grammars) of ritual magic such as the *Lemegeton (Lesser Key) of Solomon the King.* In the light of this historical literary anticipation, the Testament will be of interest to the serious student of Hermetic studies involved in the practice of the arts of magic laid down in the medieval works of the genre.

The language of the Testament's composition, New Testament Greek is influenced by a Christian hand and the original codex is a rendering from several fragmented sources; some, no doubt, oral. The appearance of several demonic entities listed by scholars of Hebrew mythology such as Asmodeus and Beelzeboul are complemented by less familiar entities such as Obyzouth, a form of Lilith, considered to be the original wife of Adam, and Ornias who torments a young man who is a favourite acolyte of King Solomon: providing the stimulus for prayer which results in the intervention of the Archangel Michael who grants the ring of power giving mastery over the demons to the Old Testament King.

In the lore of the Hermetic Qabalah, the demonic entities are held to be personifications of the unbalanced forces of the Sephiroth (emanations) of the blueprint of the Creation: a perspective which was not arrived at until the Rabbinical Qabalist Isaac Luria's revelation of the Breaking of the Vessels early in the last millennium.

Luria's work was an example of Common Era intellectual religious scholarship uniting with what can only be termed classical *revelatory philosophy* of the kind demonstrated by the approach of scholars such as Duns Scotus before the impact of the rationalists such as Aquinas and William of Occam influenced the genesis of the era of The Enlightenment.

During the pre-Augustinian age of political upheaval with the Roman Empire meeting it's ultimate point of expansion, teetering upon the brink of inevitable degeneration and impending decline, the religious spirit of enquiry was obsessed with a need to counter the chaos of temporal instability and uncertainty.

Chance and Chaos were respected as personifications of Divinity. The term Hazard was a well worn descriptive garment during the early years of the first millennium (C.E.). That is to say, the term Hazard was thought to describe not merely the possibly destructive forces of random influence that shape the destiny of both individuals and nations, but those forces which could bring winds of good fortune as easily as they might bring tidings of evil omen.

The Testament of Solomon is an early, yet erudite attempt to allegorise the taming of personifications of seemingly random, unstable forces inherent in Nature by appeal to the grace of the Higher Divinity. Consistent with the traditional dealings of the Creator with his living creations, Solomon is visited with the word of God borne by an angel: in this case - reflecting the Christian origins of the author, this is the Archangel Michael.

Just as the Book of Jubilees elevates Enoch to the status of heroic demi-god, giving him the credit for the tutelage of mankind in the documenting of wisdom in the form of written script, the *Testament of Solomon* credits it's royal author with power over the material plane of manifestation in equal measure to which his Wisdom is celebrated in the Old Testament *Book of Kings and the Book of Proverbs*.

This recognises Solomon as wearing the same mantle of immortal relevance to human affairs ascribed to other mono-mythic archetypes such as the Egyptian Thoth, the syncretic Hermes Trismegistus and the Greek Prometheus. However, Solomon's fall from divine favour is also documented within these pages as a moral fable to those easily seduced by the glamour of Earthly sensuality represented in the person of the Queen of the South (Sheba).

The Testament of Solomon is one of the very earliest surviving examples of attempts to describe a technology of enchantment that is as dependent upon the authority of the divine Creator's blessing as it is of the ability to control the powers of the eternal world employing knowledge gained through the familiarity of classification.

The naming of the 36 demonic powers of the decans is a first generation attempt to gain the Specialist's capability of control over the combinatorial factors of material influences that may be brought to bear in the area of his professional focus.

Just as the development of scientific enquiry was strengthened by the certainties provided by the organisation of known chemical elements in the coherent referencing system known as the Periodic Table of Elements from the nineteenth century onwards, the world of descriptive magical grimoires has gifted the proponents of *revelatory philosophy* with valuable tools of classification to harness in its developmental evolution.

The classical grimoires of both the late first and early second millennium (C.E.) such as the Greater and Lesser Keys of Solomon, the Sixth and Seventh Books of Moses represent the mature generation of the style of the technology of spiritual enquiry demonstrated to exist embryonically in the era of the authorship of the Testament of Solomon. Later examples of this genre, indeed the final stage into which this approach evolved include Cornelius Agrippa's *Three Books of Occult Philosophy,* Francis Barrett's *The Magus* and ultimately Crowley and Bennett's *Liber 777.*

In the tradition of the Hermetic Golden Dawn, the last 100 years have seen radical shifts in the focus of philosophy caused by advances in insights regarding the descriptive categorisations of our systems of scientific observation.

Opinions upon educational disciplines, once so immovably entrenched in the belief of the value of Behavioural drilling procedure are now informed by the notional appreciation of a wider approach inclusive of the individual's skills of cognition and capacity for self directed initiative. The focus within the science of Physics has similarly expanded to include paradigms of pure descriptive theory such as Quantum Physics and String Theory in preference to the more traditionally mechanistic models of a century ago.

Our descriptive methods of categorisation have grown more sophisticated and relativistic and the impact of such an expansion of our philosophical vocabulary has revolutionary consequences. For this reason, the age of the classic grimoires has - like classical physics passed on to be recognised as an era upon which recognisable qualities of contemporary enquiry into occult lore depend as a historical point of origin.

The Testament of Solomon is therefore offered here as a tool intended to contribute to the armoury of the New Aeon mystical enquirer.

The Testament of Solomon

1. Testament of Solomon, son of David, who was king in Jerusalem, and mastered and controlled all spirits of the air, on the earth, and under the earth. By means of them also he wrought all the transcendent works of the Temple. Telling also of the authorities they wield against men, and by what angels these demons are brought to naught. Of the sage Solomon. Blessed art thou, O Lord God, who didst give Solomon such authority. Glory to thee and might unto the ages. Amen.

2. And behold, when the Temple of the city of Jerusalem was being builded, and the artificers were working thereat, Ornias the demon came among them toward sunset; and he took away half of the pay of the chief deviser's little boy, as well as half his food. He also continued to suck the thumb of his right hand every day. And the child grew thin, although he was very much loved by the king.

3. So King Solomon called the boy one day, and questioned him, saying: "Do I not love thee more than all the artisans who are working in the Temple of God? Do I not give thee double wages and a double supply of food? How is it that day by day and hour by hour thou growest thinner?"

4. But the child said to the king: "I pray thee, O king. Listen to what has befallen all that thy child hath. After we are all released from our work on the Temple of God, after sunset, when I lie down to rest, one of the evil demons comes and takes away from me one half of my pay and one half of my food. Then he also takes hold of my right hand and sucks my thumb. And lo, my soul is oppressed, and so my body waxes thinner every day."

5. Now when I Solomon heard this, I entered the Temple of God, and prayed with all my soul, night and day, that the demon might be delivered into my hands, and that I might gain authority over him. And it came about through my prayer that grace was given to me from the Lord Sabaoth by Michael his archangel. He brought me a little ring, having a seal consisting of an engraved stone, and said to me: "Take, O Solomon, king, son of David, the gift which the Lord God has sent thee, the highest Sabaoth. With it thou shalt lock up all demons of the earth, male and female; and with their help thou shalt build up Jerusalem. But thou must wear this seal of God. And this engraving of the seal of the ring sent thee is a Pentagram."

6. And I Solomon was overjoyed, and praised and glorified the God of heaven and earth. And on the morrow I called the boy, and gave him the ring, and said to him: "take this, and at the hour in which the demon shall come unto thee, throw this ring at the chest of the demon, and say to him: 'In the name of God, King Solomon calls thee hither.' And then do thou come running to me, without having any misgivings or fear in respect of aught thou mayest hear on the part of the demon."

7. So the child took the ring, and went off; and behold, at the customary hour Ornias, the fierce demon, came like a burning fire to take the pay from the child. But the child according to the instructions received from the king, threw the ring at the chest of the demon, and said: "King Solomon calls thee hither." And then he went off at a run to the king. But the demon cried out aloud, saying: "Child, why hast thou done this to me? Take the ring off me, and I will render to thee the gold of the earth. Only take this off me, and forbear to lead me away to Solomon."

8. But the child said to the demon: "As the Lord God of Israel liveth, I will not brook thee. So come hither." And the child came at a run, rejoicing, to the king, and said: "I have brought the demon, O king, as thou didst command me, O my master. And behold, he stands before the gates of the court of thy palace, crying out, and supplicating with a loud voice; offering me the silver and gold of the earth if I will only bring him unto thee."

9. And when Solomon heard this, he rose up from his throne, and went outside into the vestibule of the court of his palace; and there he saw the demon, shuddering and trembling. And he said to him: "Who art thou?" And the demon answered: "I am called Ornias."

10. And Solomon said to him: "Tell me, O demon, to what zodiacal sign thou art subject." And he answered: "To the Water-pourer. And those who are consumed with desire for the noble virgins upon earth ... these I strangle. But in case there is no disposition to sleep, I am changed into three forms. Whenever men come to be enamoured of women, I metamorphose myself into a comely female; and I take hold of the men in their sleep, and play with them. And after a while I again take to my wings, and hide me to the heavenly regions. I also appear as a lion, and I am commanded by all the demons. I am offspring of the archangel Uriel, the power of God."

11. I Solomon, having heard the name of the archangel, prayed and glorified God, the Lord of heaven and earth. And I sealed the demon and set him to work at stone-cutting, so that he might cut the stones in the Temple, which, lying along the shore, had been brought by the Sea of Arabia. But he, fearful of the iron, continued and said to me: "I pray thee, King Solomon, let me go free; and I will bring you all the demons." And as he was not willing to be subject to me, I prayed the archangel Uriel to come and succour me; and I forthwith beheld the archangel Uriel coming down to me from the heavens.

12. And the angel bade the whales of the sea come out of the abyss. And he cast his destiny upon the ground, and that [destiny] made subject [to him] the great demon. And he commanded the great demon and bold Ornias, to cut stones at the Temple. And accordingly I Solomon glorified the God of heaven and Maker of the earth. And he bade Ornias come with his destiny, and gave him the seal, saying: "Away with thee, and bring me hither the prince of all the demons."

13. So Ornias took the finger-ring, and went off to Beelzeboul, who has kingship over the demons. He said to him: "Hither! Solomon calls thee." But Beelzeboul, having heard, said to him: "Tell me, who is this Solomon of whom thou speakest to me?" Then Ornias threw the ring at the chest of

Beelzeboul, saying: "Solomon the king calls thee." But Beelzeboul cried aloud with a mighty voice, and shot out a great burning flame of fire; and he arose, and followed Ornias, and came to Solomon.

14. And when I saw the prince of demons, I glorified the Lord God, Maker of heaven and earth, and I said: "Blessed art thou, Lord God Almighty, who hast given to Solomon thy servant wisdom, the assessor of the wise, and hast subjected unto me all the power of the devil."

15. And I questioned him, and said: "Who art thou?" The demon replied: "I am Beelzebub, the exarch of the demons. And all the demons have their chief seats close to me. And I it is who make manifest the apparition of each demon." And he promised to bring to me in bonds all the unclean spirits. And I again glorified the God of heaven and earth, as I do always give thanks to him.

16. I then asked of the demon if there were females among them. And when he told me that there were, I said that I desired to see them. So Beelzeboul went off at high speed, and brought unto me Onoskelis, that had a very pretty shape, and the skin of a fair-hued woman; and she tossed her head.

17. And when she was come, I said to her: "Tell me who art thou?" But she said to me: "I am called Onoskelis, a spirit wrought ...[Shabtai/Saturn?], lurking upon the earth. There is a golden cave where I lie. But I have a place that ever shifts. At one time I strangle men with a noose; at another, I creep up from the nature to the arms [in marg: "worms"]. But my most frequent dwelling-places are the precipices, caves, ravines. Oftentimes, however, do I consort with men in the semblance of a woman, and above all with those of a dark skin. For they share my star with me; since they it is who privily or openly worship my star, without knowing that they harm themselves, and but whet my appetite for further mischief. For they wish to provide money by means of memory (commemoration?), but I supply a little to those who worship me fairly."

18. And I Solomon questioned her about her birth, and she replied: "I was born of a voice untimely, the so called echo of a man's ordure dropped in a wood."

19. And I said to her: "Under what star dost thou pass?" And she answered me: "Under the star of the full moon, for the reason that the moon travels over most things." Then I said to her: "And what angel is it that frustrates thee?" And she said to me: "He that in thee [or "through thee"] is reigning." And I thought that she mocked me, and bade a soldier strike her. But she cried aloud, and said: "I am [subjected] to thee, O king, by the wisdom of God given to thee, and by the angel Joel."

20. So I commanded her to spin the hemp for the ropes used in the building of the house of God; and accordingly, when I had sealed and bound her, she was so overcome and brought to naught as to stand night and day spinning the hemp.

21. And I at once bade another demon to be led unto me; and instantly there approached me the demon Asmodeus, bound, and I asked him: "Who art thou?" But he shot on me a glance of anger and rage, and said: "And who art thou?" And I said to him: "Thus punished as thou art, answerest thou me?" But he, with rage, said to me: "But how shall I answer thee, for thou art a son of man; whereas I was born an angel's seed by a daughter of man, so that no word of our heavenly kind addressed to the earth-born can be overweening. Wherefore also my star is bright in heaven, and men call it, some the Wain, and some the dragon's child. I keep near unto this star. So ask me not many things; for thy kingdom also after a little time is to be disrupted, and thy glory is but for a season. And short will be thy tyranny over us; and then we shall again have free range over mankind, so as that they shall revere us as if we were gods, not knowing, men that they are, the names of the angels set over us."

22. And I Solomon, on hearing this, bound him more carefully, and ordered him to be flogged with thongs of ox-hide, and to tell me humbly what was his name and what his business. And he answered me thus: "I am called Asmodeus among mortals, and my business is to plot against the newly wedded, so that they may not know one another. And I sever them utterly by many calamities, and I waste away the beauty of virgin women, and estrange their hearts."

23. And I said to him: "Is this thy only business?" And he answered me: "I transport men into fits of madness and desire, when they have wives of their own, so that they leave them, and go off by night and day to others that belong to other men; with the result that they commit sin, and fall into murderous deeds."

24. And I adjured him by the name of the Lord Sabaôth, saying: "Fear God, Asmodeus, and tell me by what angel thou art frustrated." But he said: "By Raphael, the archangel that stands before the throne of God. But the liver and gall of a fish put me to flight, when smoked over ashes of the tamarisk." I again asked him, and said: "Hide not aught from me. For I am Solomon, son of David, King of Israel. Tell me the name of the fish which thou reverest." And he answered: "It is the Glanos by name, and is found in the rivers of Assyria; wherefore it is that I roam about in those parts."

25. And I said to him: "Hast thou nothing else about thee, Asmodeus?" And he answered: "The power of God knoweth, which hath bound me with the indissoluble bonds of yonder one's seal, that whatever I have told thee is true. I pray thee, King Solomon, condemn me not to [go into] water." But I smiled, and said to him: "As the Lord God of my fathers liveth, I will lay iron on thee to wear. But thou shalt also make the clay for the entire construction of the Temple, treading it down with thy feet." And I ordered them to give him ten water-jars to carry water in. And the demon groaned terribly, and did the work I ordered him to do. And this I did, because that fierce demon Asmodeus knew even the future. And I Solomon glorified God, who gave wisdom to me Solomon his servant. And the liver of the fish and its gall I hung on the spike of a reed, and burned it over Asmodeus because of his being so strong, and his unbearable malice was thus frustrated.

26. And I summoned again to stand before me Beelzeboul, the prince of demons, and I sat him down on a raised seat of honour, and said to him: "Why art thou alone, prince of the demons?" And he said to me: "Because I alone am left of the angels of heaven that came down. For I was first angel in the first heaven being entitled Beelzeboul. And now I control all those who are bound in Tartarus. But I too have a child, and he haunts the Red Sea. And on any suitable occasion he comes up to me again, being subject to me; and reveals to me what he has done, and I support him.

27. I Solomon said unto him: "Beelzeboul, what is thy employment?" And he answered me: "I destroy kings. I ally myself with foreign tyrants. And my own demons I set on to men, in order that the latter may believe in them and be lost. And the chosen servants of God, priests and faithful men, I excite unto desires for wicked sins, and evil heresies, and lawless deeds; and they obey me, and I bear them on to destruction. And I inspire men with envy, and [desire for] murder, and for wars and sodomy, and other evil things. And I will destroy the world."

28. So I said to him: "Bring to me thy child, who is, as thou sayest, in the Red Sea." But he said to me: "I will not bring him to thee. But there shall come to me another demon called Ephippas. Him will I bind, and he will bring him up from the deep unto me." And I said to him: "How comes thy son to be in the depth of the sea, and what is his name? "And he answered me: "Ask me not, for thou canst not learn from me. However, he will come to thee by any command, and will tell thee openly"

29. I said to him: "Tell me by what angel thou art frustrated." And he answered: "By the holy and precious name of the Almighty God, called by the

Hebrews by a row of numbers, of which the sum is 644, and among the Greeks it is Emmanuel. And if one of the Romans adjure me by the great name of the power Eleéth, I disappear at once."

30. I Solomon was astounded when I heard this; and I ordered him to saw up Theban marbles. And when he began to saw the marbles, the other demons cried out with a loud voice, howling because of their king Beelzeboul.

31. But I Solomon questioned him, saying: "If thou wouldst gain a respite, discourse to me about the things in heaven." And Beelzeboul said: "Hear, O king, if thou burn gum, and incense, and bulb of the sea, with nard and saffron, and light seven lamps in an earthquake, thou wilt firmly fix thy house. And if, being pure, thou light them at dawn in the sun alight, then wilt thou see the heavenly dragons, how they wind themselves along and drag the chariot of the sun."

32. And I Solomon, having heard this, rebuked him, and said: "Silence for this present, and continue to saw the marbles as I commanded thee." And I Solomon praised God, and commanded another demon to present himself to me. And one came before me who carried his face high up in the air, but the rest of the spirit curled away like a snail. And it broke through the few soldiers, and raised also a terrible dust on the ground, and carried it upwards; and then again hurled it back to frighten us, and asked what questions I could ask as a rule. And I stood up, and spat on the ground in that spot, and sealed with the ring of God.

And forthwith the dust-wind stopped. Then I asked him, saying: "Who art thou, O wind?" Then he once more shook up a dust, and answered me: "What wouldst thou have, King Solomon?" I answered him: "Tell me what thou art called, and I would fain ask thee a question. But so far I give thanks to God who has made me wise to answer their evil plots."

33. But [the demon] answered me: "I am the spirit of the ashes (Tephras)." And I said to him: "What is thy pursuit?" And he said: "I bring darkness on men, and set fire to fields; and I bring homesteads to naught. But most busy am I in summer. However, when I get an opportunity, I creep into corners of the wall, by night and day. For I am offspring of the great one, and nothing less." Accordingly I said to him: "Under what star dost thou lie?" And he answered: "In the very tip of the moon's horn, when it is found in the south. There is my star. For I have been bidden to restrain the convulsions of the hemitertian fever; and this is why many men pray to the hemitertian fever, using these three names: Bultala, Thallal, Melchal. And I heal them." And I said to him: "I am Solomon; when therefore thou wouldst do harm, by whose aid dost thou do it?" But he said to me: "By the angel's, by whom also the third day's fever is lulled to rest." So I questioned him, and said: "And by what name?" And he answered: "That of the archangel Azael." And I summoned the archangel Azael, and set a seal on the demon, and commanded him to seize great stones, and toss them up to the workmen on the higher parts of the Temple. And, being compelled, the demon began to do what he was bidden to do.

34. And I glorified God afresh who gave me this authority, and ordered another demon to come before me. And there came seven spirits, females, bound and woven together, fair in appearance and comely. And I Solomon, seeing them, questioned them and said: "Who are ye?" But they, with one accord, said with one voice: "We are of the thirty-three elements of the cosmic ruler of the darkness." And the first said: "I am Deception." The second said: "I am Strife." The third: "I am Klothod, which is battle." The fourth: "I am Jealousy." The fifth: "I am Power." The sixth: "I am Error." The seventh: "I am the worst of all, and our stars are in heaven. Seven stars humble in sheen, and all together. And we are called as it were goddesses. We change our place all and together, and together we live, sometimes in Lydia, sometimes in Olympus, sometimes in a great mountain."

35. So I Solomon questioned them one by one, beginning with the first, and going down to the seventh. The first said: "I am Deception, I deceive and weave snares here and there. I whet and excite heresies. But I have an angel who frustrates me, Lamechalal."

36. Likewise also the second said: "I am Strife, strife of strifes. I bring timbers, stones, hangers, my weapons on the spot. But I have an angel who frustrates me, Baruchiachel."

37. Likewise also the third said: "I am called Klothod, which is Battle, and I cause the well-behaved to scatter and fall foul one of the other. And why do I say so much? I have an angel that frustrates me: "Marmarath."

38. Likewise also the fourth said: "I cause men to forget their sobriety and moderation. I part them and split them into parties; for Strife follows me hand in hand. I rend the husband from the sharer of his bed, and children from parents, and brothers from sisters.

But why tell so much to my despite? I have an angel that

frustrates me, the great Balthial."

39. Likewise also the fifth said: "I am Power. By power I raise up tyrants and tear down kings. To all rebels I furnish power. I have an angel that frustrates me, Asteraôth."

40. Likewise also the sixth said: "I am Error, O King Solomon. And I will make thee to err, as I have before made thee to err, when I caused thee to slay thy own brother. I will lead you into error, so as to pry into graves [3]; and 1 teach them that dig, and I lead errant souls away from all piety, and many other evil traits are mine. But I have an angel that frustrates me, Uriel."

41. Likewise also the seventh said: "I am the worst, and I make thee worse off than thou wast; because I will impose the bonds of Artemis. But the locust will set me free, for by means thereof is it fated that thou shalt achieve my desire [...]. For if one were wise, he would not turn his steps toward me."

42. So I Solomon, having heard and wondered, sealed them with my ring; and since they were so considerable, I bade them dig the foundations of the Temple of God. For the length of it was 250 cubits. And I bade them be industrious, and with one murmur of joint protest they began to perform the tasks enjoined.

43. But I Solomon glorified the Lord, and bade another demon come before me. And there was brought to me a demon having all the limbs of a man, but without a head. And I, seeing him, said to him: "Tell me, who art thou?" And he answered: "I am a demon." So I said to him: "Which?" And he answered me: "I am called Envy. For I delight to devour heads, being desirous to secure for myself a head; but I do not eat enough, but am anxious to have such a head as thou hast."

44. I Solomon, on hearing this, sealed him, stretching out my hand against his chest. Whereon the demon leapt up, and threw himself down, and gave a groan, saying: "Woe is me! where am I come to? O traitor Ornias, I cannot see!" So I said to him: "I am Solomon. Tell me then how thou dost manage to see." And he answered me: "By means of my feelings." I then, Solomon, having heard his voice come up to me, asked him how he managed to speak. And he answered me:

"I, O King Solomon, am wholly voice, for I have inherited the voices of many men. For in the case of all men who are called dumb, I it is who smashed their heads, when they were children and had reached their eighth day.

Then when a child is crying in the night, I become a spirit, and glide by means of his voice [...]. In the crossways also I have many services to render, and my encounter is fraught with harm. For I grasp in all instant a man's head, and with my hands, as with a sword, I cut it off, and put it on to myself. And in this way, by means of the fire which is in me, through my neck it is swallowed up. I it is that sends grave mutilations and incurable on men's feet, and inflict sores."

45. And I Solomon, on hearing this, said to him: "Tell me how thou dost discharge forth the fire? Out of what sources dost thou emit it?" And the spirit said to me: "From the Day-star. For here hath not yet been found that Elburion, to whom men offer prayers and kindle lights. And his name is invoked by the seven demons before me. And he cherishes them."
46. But I said to him: "Tell me his name." But he answered: "I cannot tell thee. For if I tell his name, I render myself incurable. But he will come in response to his name." And on hearing this, I Solomon said to him: "Tell me then, by what angel thou art frustrated?" And he answered: "By the fiery

flash of lightning." And I bowed myself before the Lord God of Israel, and bade him remain in the keeping of Beelzeboul until Iax the Angelic Watcher should come.

47. Then I ordered another demon to come before me, and there came into my presence a hound, having a very large shape, and it spoke with a loud voice, and said, "Hail, Lord, King Solomon!" And I Solomon was astounded. I said to it: Who art thou, O hound?" And it answered: "I do indeed seem to thee to be a hound, but before thou wast, O King Solomon, I was a man that wrought many unholy deeds on earth. I was surpassingly learned in letters, and was so mighty that I could hold the stars of heaven back. And many divine works did I prepare. For I do harm to men who follow after our star, and turn them to [...]. And I seize the frenzied men by the larynx, and so destroy them."

48. And I Solomon said to him: "What is thy name?" And he answered: "Staff" (Rabdos). And I said to him: "What is thine employment? And what results canst thou achieve?" And he replied: "Give me thy man, and I will lead him away into a mountainous spot, and will show him a green stone tossed to and fro, with which thou mayest adorn the temple of the Lord God."

49. And I Solomon, on hearing this, ordered my servant to set off with him, and to take the finger-ring bearing the seal of God with him. And I said to him: "Whoever shall show thee the green stone, seal him with this finger-ring. And mark the spot with care, and bring me the demon hither. And the demon showed him the green stone, and he sealed it, and brought the demon to me. And I Solomon decided to confine with my seal on my right hand the two, the headless demon, likewise the hound, that was so huge; he should be bound as well. And I bade the hound keep safe the fiery spirit so that lamps as it were might by day and night cast their light through its maw on the artisans at work.

50. And I Solomon took from the mine of that stone 200 shekels for the supports of the table of incense, which was similar in appearance. And I Solomon glorified the Lord God, and then closed round the treasure of that stone. And I ordered afresh the demons to cut marble for the construction of the house of God. And I Solomon prayed to the Lord, and asked the hound, saying: "By what angel art thou frustrated?" And the demon replied: "By the great Brieus."

51. And I praised the Lord God of heaven and earth, and bade another demon come forward to me; and there came before me one in the form of a lion roaring. And he stood and answered me saying: "O king, in the form which I have, I am a spirit quite incapable of being perceived. Upon all men who lie prostrate with sickness I leap, coming stealthily along; and I render the man weak, so that his habit of body is enfeebled. But I have also another glory, O king. I cast out demons, and I have legions under my control. And I am capable of being received in my dwelling-places, along with all the demons belonging to the legions under me." But I Solomon, on hearing this, asked him: "What is thy name?" But he answered: "Lion bearer, Rath in kind." And I said to him: "How art thou to be frustrated along with thy legions? What angel is it that frustrates thee?" And he answered: "If I tell thee my name, I bind not myself alone, but also the legions of demons under me."

52. So I said to him: "I adjure thee in the name of the God Sabaoth, to tell me by what name thou art frustrated along with thy host." And the spirit answered me: "The 'great among men,' who is to suffer many things at the hands of men, whose name is the figure 644, which is Emmanuel; he it is who has bound us, and who will then come and plunge us from the steep under water. He is noised abroad in the three letters which bring him down."

53. And I Solomon, on hearing this, glorified God, and condemned his legion to carry wood from the thicket. And I condemned the lion-shaped one himself to saw up the wood small with his teeth, for burning in the unquenchable furnace for the Temple of God.

54. And I worshipped the Lord God of Israel, and bade another demon come forward. And there came before me a dragon, three-headed, of fearful hue. And I questioned him: "Who art thou?" And he answered me: "I am a caltrop-like spirit, whose activity in three lines. But I blind children in women's wombs, and twirl their ears round. And I make them deaf and mute. And I have again in my third head means of slipping in. And I smite men in the limbless part of the body, and cause them to fall down, and foam, and grind their teeth. But I have my own way of being frustrated, Jerusalem being signified in writing, unto the place called 'of the head." For there is fore-appointed the angel of the great counsel, and now he will openly dwell on the cross. He doth frustrate me, and to him am I subject."

55. "But in the place where thou sittest, O King Solomon, standeth a column in the air, of purple... The demon called Ephippas hath brought [it] up from the Red Sea, from inner Arabia. He it is that shall be shut up in a skin-bottle and brought before thee. But at the entrance of the Temple, which thou hast begun to build, O King Solomon, lies stored much gold, which dig thou up and carry off." And I Solomon sent my servant, and found it to be as the demon told me. And I sealed him with my ring, and praised the Lord God."

56. So I said to him: "What art thou called?" And the demon said: "I am the crest of dragons." And I bade him make bricks in the Temple. He had human hands.

57. And I adored the Lord God of Israel, and bade another demon present himself. And there came before me a spirit in woman's form, that had a head without any limbs, and her hair was dishevelled. And I said to her: "Who art thou?" But she answered: "Nay, who art thou? And why dost thou want to hear concerning me? But, as thou wouldst learn, here I stand bound before thy face. Go then into thy royal storehouses and wash thy hands. Then sit down afresh before thy tribunal, and ask me questions; and thou shalt learn, O king, who I am."

58. And I Solomon did as she enjoined me, and restrained myself because of the wisdom dwelling in me; in order that I might hear of her deeds, and reprehend them, and manifest them to men. And I sat down, and said to the demon: "What art thou?" And she said: "I am called among men Obizuth; and by night I sleep not, but go my rounds over all the world, and visit women in childbirth. And divining the hour I take my stand; and if I am lucky, I strangle the child. But if not, I retire to another place. For I cannot for a single night retire unsuccessful. For I am a fierce spirit, of myriad names and many shapes. And now hither, now thither I roam. And to westering parts I go my rounds. But as it now is, though thou hast sealed me round with the ring of God, thou hast done nothing. I am not standing before thee, and thou wilt not be able to command me. For I have no work other than the destruction of children, and the making their ears to be deaf, and the working of evil to their eyes, and the binding their mouths with a bond, and the ruin of their minds, and paining of their bodies."

59. When I Solomon heard this, I marvelled at her appearance, for I beheld all her body to be in darkness. But her glance was altogether bright and greeny, and her hair was tossed wildly like a dragon's; and the whole of her limbs were invisible. And her voice was very clear as it came to me. And I cunningly said: "Tell me by what angel thou art frustrated, O evil spirit?" By she answered me: "By the angel of God called Afarôt, which is interpreted Raphael, by whom I am frustrated now and for all time. His name, if any man know it, and write the same on a woman in childbirth, then I shall not be able to enter her. Of this name the number is 640." And I Solomon having heard this, and having glorified the Lord, ordered her hair to be bound, and that she should be hung up in front of the Temple of God; that all the children of Israel, as they passed, might see it, and glorify the Lord God of Israel, who had given me this authority, with wisdom and power from God, by means of this signet.

60. And I again ordered another demon to come before me. And the came, rolling itself along, one in appearance like to a dragon, but having the face and hands of a man. And all its limbs, except the feet, were those of a dragon; and it had wings on its back. And when I beheld it, I was astonished, and said: "Who art thou, demon, and what art thou called? And whence hast thou come? Tell me."

61. And the spirit answered and said: "This is the first time I have stood before the, O King Solomon. I am a spirit made into a god among men, but now brought to naught by the ring and wisdom vouchsafed to thee by God. Now I am the so-called winged dragon, and I chamber not with many women, but only with a few that are of fair shape, which possess the name of xuli, of this star. And I pair with them in the guise of a spirit winged in form, coitum habens per nates. And she on whom I have leapt goes heavy with child, and that which is born of her becomes Eros. But since such offspring cannot be carried by men, the woman in question breaks wind. Such is my role. Supposed then only that I am satisfied, and all the other demons molested and disturbed by thee will speak the whole truth. But those composed of fire will cause to be burned up by fire the material of the logs which is to be collected by them for the building in the Temple."

62. And as the demon said this, I saw the spirit going forth from his mouth, and it consumed the wood of the frankincense-tree, and burned up all the logs which we had placed in the Temple of God. And I Solomon saw what the spirit had done, and I marvelled.

63. And, having glorified God, I asked the dragon-shaped demon, and said: "Tell me, by what angel art thou frustrated?" And he answered: "By the great angel which has its seat in the second heaven, which is called in Hebrew Bazazeth. And I Solomon, having heard this, and having invoked his angel, condemned him to saw up marbles for the building of the Temple of God; and I praised God, and commanded another demon to come before me.

64. And there came before my face another spirit, as it were a woman in the form she had. But on her shoulders she had two other heads with hands. And I asked her, and said: "Tell me, who art thou?" And she said to me: "I am Enêpsigos, who also have a myriad names." And I said her: "By what angel art thou frustrated?" But she said to me: "What seekest, what askest thou? I undergo changes, like the goddess I am called. And I change again, and pass into possession of another shape. And be not desirous therefore to know all that concerns me. But since thou art before me for this much, hearken. I have my abode in the moon, and for that reason I possess three forms. At times I am magically invoked by the wise as Kronos. At other times, in connexion with those who bring me down, I come down and appear in another shape. The measure of the element is inexplicable and indefinable, and not to be frustrated. I then, changing into these three forms, come down and become such as thou seest me; but I am frustrated by the angel Rathanael, who sits in the third heaven. This then is why I speak to thee. Yonder temple cannot contain me."

65. I therefore Solomon prayed to my God, and I invoked the angel of whom Enépsigos spoke to me, and used my seal. And I sealed her with a triple chain, and (placed) beneath her the fastening of the chain. I used the seal of God, and the spirit prophesied to me, saying: "This is what thou, King Solomon, doest to us. But after a time thy kingdom shall be broken, and again in season this Temple shall be riven asunder; and all Jerusalem shall be undone by the King of the Persians and Medes and Chaldaeans. And the vessels of this Temple, which thou makest, shall be put to servile uses of the gods; and along with them all the jars, in which thou dost shut us up, shall be broken by the hands of men. And then we shall go forth in great power hither and thither, and be disseminated all over the world. And we shall lead astray the inhabited world for a long season, until the Son of God is stretched upon the cross. For never before doth arise a king like unto him, one frustrating us all, whose mother shall not have contact with man. Who else can receive such authority over spirits, except he, whom the first devil will seek to tempt, but will not prevail over? The number of his name is 644, which is Emmanuel. Wherefore, O King Solomon, thy time is evil, and thy years short and evil, and to thy servant shall thy kingdom be given."

66. And I Solomon, having heard this, glorified God. And though I marvelled at the apology of the demons, I did not credit it until it came true. And I did not believe their words; but when they were realized, then I understood, and at my death I wrote this Testament to the children of Israel, and gave it to them, so that they might know the powers of the demons and their shapes, and the names of their angels, by which these angels are frustrated. And I glorified the Lord God of Israel, and commanded the spirits to be bound with bonds indissoluble.

67. And having praised God, I commanded another spirit to come before me; and there came before my face another demon, having in front the shape of a horse, but behind of a fish. And he had a mighty voice, and said to me: "O King Solomon, I am a fierce spirit of the sea, and I am greedy of gold and silver. I am such a spirit as rounds itself and comes over the expanses of the water of the sea, and I trip up the men who sail thereon. For I round myself into a wave, and transform myself, and then throw myself on ships and come right in on them. And that is my business, and my way of getting hold of money and men. For I take the men, and whirl them round with myself, and hurl the men out of the sea. For I am not covetous of men's bodies, but cast them up out of the sea so far. But since Beelzeboul, ruler of the spirits of air and of those under the earth, and lord of earthly ones, hath a joint kingship with us in respect of the deeds of each one of us, therefore I went up from the sea, to get a certain outlook in his company.

68. "But I also have another character and role. I metamorphose myself into waves, and come up from the sea. And I show myself to men, so that those on earth call me Kunos Paston, because I assume the human form. And my name is a true one. For by my passage up into men, I send forth a certain nausea. I came then to take counsel with the prince Beelzeboul; and he bound me and delivered me into thy hands. And I am here before thee because of this seal, and thou dost now torment me. Behold now, in two or three days the spirit that converseth with thee will fail, because I shall have no water."

69. And I said to him: "Tell me by what angel thou art frustrated." And he answered: "By Iameth." And I glorified God. I commanded the spirit to be thrown into a phial along with ten jugs of sea-water of two measures each. And I sealed them round above the marbles and asphalt and pitch in the mouth of the vessel. And having sealed it with my ring, I ordered it to be deposited in the Temple of God. And I ordered another spirit to come before me.

70. And there came before my face another enslaved spirit, having obscurely the form of a man, with gleaming eyes, and bearing in his hand a blade. And I asked: "Who art thou? But he answered: "I am a lascivious spirit, engendered of a giant man who dies in the massacre in the time of the giants." I said to him: "Tell me what thou art employed on upon earth, and where thou hast thy dwelling."

71. And he said: "My dwelling is in fruitful places, but my procedure is this. I seat myself beside the men who pass along among the tombs, and in untimely season I assume the form of the dead; and if I catch any one, I at once destroy him with my sword. But if I cannot destroy him, I cause him to be possessed with a demon, and to devour his own flesh, and the hair to fall off his chin." But I said to him: "Do thou then be in fear of the God of heaven and of earth, and tell me by angel thou art frustrated." And he answered: "He destroys me who is to become Saviour, a man whose number, if any one shall write it on his forehead, he will defeat me, and in fear I shall quickly retreat. And, indeed, if any one write this sign on him, I shall be in fear." And I Solomon, on hearing this, and having glorified the Lord God, shut up this demon like the rest.

72. And I commanded another demon to come before me. And there came before my face thirty-six spirits, their heads shapeless like dogs, but in themselves they were human in form; with faces of asses, faces of oxen, and faces of birds. And I Solomon, on hearing and seeing them, wondered, and I asked them and said: "Who are you?" But they, of one accord with one voice, said: "We are the thirty-six elements, the world-rulers of this darkness. But, O King Solomon, thou wilt not wrong us nor imprison us, nor lay command on us; but since the Lord God has given thee authority over every spirit, in the air, and on the earth, and under the earth, therefore do we also present ourselves before thee like the other spirits, from ram and bull, from [35] both twin and crab, lion and virgin, scales and scorpion, archer, goat-horned, water pourer, and fish.

73. Then I Solomon invoked the name of the Lord Sabaoth, and questioned each in turn as to what was its character. And I bade each one come forward and tell of its actions. Then the first one came forward, and said: "I am the first decans of the zodiacal circle, and I am called the ram, and with me are these two." So I put to them the question:

"Who are ye called?" The first said: "I, O Lord, am called Ruax, and I cause the heads of men to be idle, and I pillage their brows. But let me only hear the words, 'Michael, imprison Ruax,' and at once I retreat."

74. And the second said: "I am called Barsafael, and I cause those who are subject to my hour to feel the pain of migraine. If only I hear the words, 'Gabriel, imprison Barsafael,' at once I retreat."

75. The third said: "I am called Arôtosael. I do harm to eyes, and grievously injure them. Only let me hear the words, 'Uriel, imprison Aratosael' (sic), at once I retreat . . . "

76. The fifth said: "I am called Iudal, and I bring about a block in the ears and deafness of hearing. If I hear, 'Uruel Iudal,' I at once retreat."

77. The sixth said: "I am called Sphendonaêl. I cause tumours of the parotid gland, and inflammations of the tonsils, and tetanic recurvation. If I hear, 'Sabrael, imprison Sphendonaêl,' at once I retreat."

78. And the Seventh said: "I am called Sphandôr, and I weaken the strength of the shoulders, and cause them to tremble; and I paralyze the nerves of the hands, and I break and bruise the bones of the neck. And I, I suck out the marrow. But if I hear the words, 'Araêl, imprison Sphandôr,' I at once retreat."

79. And the eight said: "I am called Belbel. I distort the hearts and minds of men. If I hear the words, 'Araêl, imprison Belbel,' I at once retreat."

80. And the ninth said: "I am called Kurtaêl. I send colics in the bowels. I induce pains. If I hear the words, 'Iaôth, imprison Kurtaêl,' I at once retreat."

81. The tenth said: "I am called Metathiax. I cause the reins to ache. If I hear the words, 'Adônaêl, imprison Metathiax,' I at once retreat."

82. The eleventh said: "I am called Katanikotaêl. I create strife and wrongs in men's homes, and send on them hard temper. If any one would be at peace in his home, let him write on seven leaves of laurel the name of the angel that frustrates me, along with these names: Iae, Ieô, sons of Sabaôth, in the name of the great God let him shut up Katanikotaêl. Then let him wash the laurel-leaves in water, and sprinkle his house with the water, from within to the outside. And at once I retreat"

83. The twelfth said: "I am called Saphathoraél, and I inspire partisanship in men, and delight in causing them to stumble. If any one will write on paper these names of angels, Iacô, Iealô, Iôelet, Sabaôth, Ithoth, Bae, and having folded it up, wear it round his neck or against his ear, I at once retreat and dissipate the drunken fit."

84. The thirteenth said: "I am called Bobêl (sic), and I cause nervous illness by my assaults. If I hear the name of the great 'Adonaêl, imprison Bothothêl,' I at once retreat."

85. The fourteenth said: "I am called Kumeatêl, and I inflict shivering fits and torpor. If only I hear the words: 'Zôrôêl, imprison Kumentaêl,' I at once retreat."

86. The fifteenth said: "I am called Roêlêd. I cause cold and frost and pain in the stomach. Let me only hear the words: 'Iax, bide not, be not warmed, for Solomon is fairer than eleven fathers,' I at [once] retreat."

87. The sixteenth said: "I am called Atrax. I inflict upon men fevers, irremediable and harmful. If you would imprison me, chop up coriander and smear it on the lips, reciting the following charm: 'The fever which is from dirt. I exorcise thee by the throne of the most high God, retreat from dirt and retreat from the creature fashioned by God.' And at once I retreat."

88. The seventeenth said: "I am called Ieropaêl. On the stomach of men I sit, and cause convulsions in the bath and in the road; and wherever I be found, or find a man, I throw him down. But if any one will say to the afflicted into their ear these names, three times over, into the right ear: 'Iudarizê, Sabunê, Denôê,' I at once retreat"

89. The eighteenth said: "I am called Buldumêch. I separate wife from husband and bring about a grudge between them. If any one write down the names of thy sires, Solomon, on paper and place it in the antechamber of his house, I retreat thence. And the legend written shall be as follows: 'The God of Abram, and the God of Isaac, and the God of Jacob commands thee -- retire from this house in peace.' And I at once retire."

90. The nineteenth said: "I am called Naôth, and I take my seat on the knees of men. If any one write on paper: 'Phnunoboêol, depart Nathath, and touch thou not the neck,' I at once retreat.

91. The twentieth said: "I am called Marderô. I send on men incurable fever. If any one write on the leaf of a book: 'Sphênêr, Rafael, retire, drag me not about, flay me not,' and tie it round his neck, I at once retreat."

92. The twenty-first said: "I am called Alath, and I cause coughing and hard-breathing in children. If any one write on paper: 'Rorêx, do thou pursue Alath,' and fasten it round his neck, I at once retire..."

93. The twenty-third said: "I am called Nefthada. I cause the reins to ache, and I bring about dysury. If any one write on a plate of tin the words: 'Iathôth, Uruêl, Nephthada,' and fasten it round the loins, I at once retreat."

94. The twenty-fourth said: "I am called Akton. I cause ribs and lumbic muscles to ache. If one engrave on copper material, taken from a ship which has missed its anchorage, this: 'Marmaraôth, Sabaôth, pursue Akton,' and fasten it round the loin, I at once retreat."

95. The twenty-fifth said: "I am called Anatreth, and I rend burnings and fevers into the entrails. But if I hear: 'Arara, Charara,' instantly do I retreat."

96. The twenty-sixth said: "I am called Enenuth. I steal away men's minds, and change their hearts, and make a man toothless (?). If one write: 'Allazoôl, pursue Enenuth,' and tie the paper round him, I at once retreat."

97. The twenty-seventh said: "I am called Phêth. I make men consumptive and cause hemorrhagia. ,If one exorcise me in wine, sweet-smelling and unmixed by the eleventh aeon, and say: 'I exorcise thee by the eleventh aeon to stop, I demand, Phêth (Axiôphêth),' then give it to the patient to drink, and I at once retreat."

98. The twenty-eighth said: "I am called Harpax, and I send sleeplessness on men. If one write 'Kokphnêdismos,' and bind it round the temples, I at once retire."

99. The twenty-ninth said: "I am called Anostêr. I engender uterine mania and pains in the bladder. If one powder into pure oil three seeds of laurel and smear it on, saying: 'I exorcise thee, Anostêr. Stop by Marmaraô,' at once I retreat."

100. The thirtieth said: "I am called Alleborith. If in eating fish one has swallowed a bone, then he must take a bone from the fish and cough, and at once I retreat."

101. The thirty-first said: "I am called Hephesimireth, and cause lingering disease. If you throw salt, rubbed in the hand, into oil and smear it on the patient, saying: 'Seraphim, Cherubim, help me!' I at once retire."

102. The thirty-second said: "I am called Ichthion. I paralyze muscles and contuse them. If I hear 'Adonaêth, help!' I at once retire."

103. The thirty-third said: "I am called Agchoniôn. I lie among swaddling-clothes and in the precipice. And if any one write on fig-leaves 'Lycurgos,' taking away one letter at a time, and write it, reversing the letters, I retire at once. 'Lycurgos, ycurgos, kurgos, yrgos, gos, os.'"

104. The thirty-fourth said: "I am called Autothith. I cause grudges and fighting. Therefore I am frustrated by Alpha and Omega, if written down."

105. The thirty-fifth said: "I am called Phthenoth. I cast evil eye on every man. Therefore, the eye much suffering, if it be drawn. frustrates me."

106. The thirty-sixth said: "I am called Bianakith. I have a grudge against the body. I lay waste houses, I cause flesh to decay, and all else that is similar. If a man write on the front-door of his house: 'Mêltô, Ardu, Anaath,' I flee from that place."

107. And I Solomon, when I heard this, glorified the God of heaven and earth. And I commanded them to fetch water in the Temple of God. And I furthermore prayed to the Lord God to cause the demons without, that hamper humanity, to be bound and made to approach the Temple of God. Some of these demons I condemned to do the heavy work of the construction of the Temple of God. Others I shut up in prisons. Others I ordered to wrestle with fire in (the making of) gold and silver, sitting down by lead and spoon. And to make ready places for the other demons in which they should be confined.

108. And I Solomon had much quiet in all the earth, and spent my life in profound peace, honoured by all men and by all under heaven. And I built the entire Temple of the Lord God. And my kingdom was prosperous, and my army was with me. And for the rest the city of Jerusalem had repose, rejoicing and delighted. And all the kings of the earth came to me from the ends of the earth to behold the Temple which I builded to the Lord God. And having heard of the wisdom given to me, they did homage to me in the Temple, bringing gold and silver and precious stones, many and divers, and bronze, and iron, and lead, and cedar logs. And woods decay not they brought me, for the equipment of the Temple of God.

109. And among them also the queen of the South, being a witch, came in great concern and bowed low before me to the earth. And having heard my wisdom, she glorified the God of Israel, and she made formal trial of all my wisdom, of all love in which I instructed her, according to the wisdom imparted to me. And all the sons of Israel glorified God.

110. And behold, in those days one of the workmen, of ripe old age, threw himself down before me, and said: "King Solomon, pity me, because I am old." So I bade him stand up, and said: "Tell me, old man, all you will." And he answered: "I beseech you king, I have an only-born son, and he insults and beats me openly, and plucks out the hair of my head, and threatens me with a painful death. Therefore I beseech you avenge me.

111. And I Solomon, on hearing this, felt compunction as I looked at his old age; and I bade the child be brought to me. And when he was brought I questioned him whether it were true. And the youth said: "I was not so filled with madness as to strike my father with my hand. Be kind to me, O king. For I have not dared to commit such impiety, poor wretch that I am."

But I Solomon on hearing this from the youth, exhorted the old man to reflect on the matter, and accept his son's apology. However, he would not, but said he would rather let him die. And as the old man would not yield, I was about to pronounce sentence on the youth, when I saw Ornias the demon laughing. I was very angry at the demon's laughing in my presence; and I ordered my men to remove the other parties, and bring forward Ornias before my tribunal.

And when he was brought before me, I said to him: "Accursed one, why didst thou look at me and laugh?" And the demon answered: "Prithee, king, it was not because of thee I laughed, but because of this ill-starred old man and the wretched youth, his son. For after three days his son will die untimely; and lo, the old man desires to foully make away with him."

112. But I Solomon, having heard this, said to the demon: "Is that true that thou speakest?" And he answered: "It is true; O king." And I, on hearing that, bade them remove the demon, and that they should again bring before me the old man with his son. I bade them make friends with one another again, and I supplied them with food. And then I told the old man after three days to bring his son again to me here; "and," said I, "I will attend to him." And they saluted me, and went their way.

113. And when they were gone I ordered Ornias to be brought forward, and said to him: "Tell me how you know this;" and he answered: "We demons ascend into the firmament of heaven, and fly about among the stars.

"And we hear the sentences which go forth upon the souls of men, and forthwith we come, and whether by force of influence, or by fire, or by sword, or by some accident, we veil our act of destruction; and if a man does not die by some untimely disaster or by violence, then we demons transform ourselves in such a way as to appear to men and be worshipped in our human nature."

114. I therefore, having heard this, glorified the Lord God, and again I questioned the demon, saying: "Tell me how ye can ascend into heaven, being demons, and amidst the stars and holy angels intermingle." And he answered: "Just as things are fulfilled in heaven, so also on earth (are fulfilled) the types of all of them. For there are principalities, authorities, world-rulers, and we demons fly about in the air; and we hear the voices of the heavenly beings, and survey all the powers. And as having no ground (basis) on which to alight and rest, we lose strength and fall off like leaves from trees. And men seeing us imagine that the stars are falling from heaven. But it is not really so, O king; but we fall because of our weakness, and because we have nowhere anything to lay hold of; and so we fall down like lightnings [3] in the depth of night and suddenly. And we set cities in flames and fire the fields. For the stars have firm foundations in the heavens like the sun and the moon."

115. And I Solomon, having heard this, ordered the demon to be guarded for five days. And after the five days I recalled the old man, and was about to question him. But he came to me in grief and with black face. And I said to him: "Tell me, old man, where is thy son? And what means this garb?" And he answered: "Lo, I am become childless, and sit by my son's grave in despair. For it is already two days that he is dead." But I Solomon, on hearing that, and knowing that the demon Ornias had told me the truth, glorified the God of Israel.

116. And the queen of the South saw all this, and marvelled, [41] glorifying the God of Israel; and she beheld the Temple of the Lord being builded. And she gave a siklos of gold and one hundred myriads of silver and choice bronze, and she went into the Temple. And (she beheld) the altar of incense and the brazen supports of this altar, and the gems of the lamps flashing forth of different colours, and of the lamp stand of stone, and of emerald, and hyacinth, and sapphire; and she beheld the vessels of gold, and silver, and bronze, and wood, and the folds of skins dyed red with madder. And she saw the bases of the pillars of the Temple of the Lord. All were of one gold ... apart from the demons whom I condemned to labour. And there was peace in the circle of my kingdom and over all the earth.

117. And it came to pass, which I was in my kingdom, the King of the Arabians, Adares, sent me a letter, and the writing of the letter was written as follows: -- "To King Solomon, all hail! Lo, we have heard, and it hath been heard unto all the ends of the earth, concerning the wisdom vouchsafed in thee, and that thou art a man merciful from the Lord. And understanding hath been granted thee over all the spirits of the air, and on earth, and under the earth.

"Now, forasmuch as there is present in the land of Arabia a spirit of the following kind: at early dawn there begins to blow a certain wind until the third hour. And its blast is harsh and terrible, and it slays man and beast. And no spirit can live upon earth against this demon. I pray thee then, forasmuch as the spirit is a wind, contrive something according to the wisdom given in thee by the Lord thy God, and deign to send a man able to capture it. And behold, King Solomon, I and my people and all my land will serve thee unto death. And all Arabia shall be at peace with thee, if thou wilt perform this act of righteousness for us. Wherefore we pray thee, contemn not our humble prayer, and suffer not to be utterly brought to naught the eparchy subordinated to thy authority. Because we are suppliants, both I and my people and all my land. Farewell to my Lord. All health!"

118. And I Solomon read this epistle; and I folded it up and gave it to my people, and said to them: "After seven days shalt thou remind me of this epistle. And Jerusalem was built, and the Temple was being completed. And there was a stone, the end stone of the corner lying there, great, chosen out, one which I desired lay in the head of the corner of the completion of the Temple. And all the workmen, and all the demons helping them came to the same place to bring up the stone and lay it on the pinnacle of the holy Temple, and were not strong enough to stir it, and lay it upon the corner allotted to it. For that stone was exceedingly great and useful for the corner of the Temple."

119. And after seven days, being reminded of the epistle of Adares, King of Arabia, I called my servant and said to him: "Order thy camel and take for thyself a leather flask, and take also this seal. And go away into Arabia to the place in which the evil spirit blows; and there take the flask, and the signet-ring in front of the mouth of the flask, and (hold them) towards the blast of the spirit. And when the flask is blown out, thou wilt understand that the demon is (in it). Then hastily tie up the mouth of to flask, and seal it securely with the seal-ring, and lay it carefully on the camel and bring it me hither. And if on the way it offer thee gold or silver or treasure in return for letting it go, see that thou be not persuaded. But arrange without using oath to release it. And then if it point out to the places where are gold or silver, mark the places and seal them with this seal. And bring the demon to me. And now depart, and fare thee well."

120. Then the youth did as was bidden him. And he ordered his camel, and laid on it a flask, and set off into Arabia. And the men of that region would not believe that he would be able to catch the evil spirit. And when it was dawn, the servant stood before the spirit's blast, and laid the flask on the ground, and the finger-ring on the mouth of the flask. And the demon blew through the middle of the finger-ring into the mouth of the flask, and going in blew out the flask. But the man promptly stood up to it and drew tight with his hand the mouth of the flask, in the name of the Lord God of Sabaôth. And the demon remained within the flask. And after that the youth remained in that land three days to make trial. And the spirit no longer blew against that city. And all the Arabs knew that he had safely shut in the spirit.

121. Then the youth fastened the flask on the camel, and the Arabs sent him forth on his way with much honour and precious gifts, praising and magnifying the God of Israel. But the youth brought in the bag and laid it in the middle of the Temple. And on the next day, I King Solomon, went into the Temple of God and sat in deep distress about the stone of the end of the corner. And when I entered the Temple, the flask stood up and walked around some seven steps and then fell on its mouth and did homage to me. And I marvelled that even along with the bottle the demon still had power and could walk about; and I commanded it to stand up. And the flask stood up, and stood on its feet all blown out. And I questioned him, saying: "Tell me, who art thou?" And the spirit within said: "I am the demon called Ephippas, that is in Arabia." And I said to him: "Is this thy name?" And he answered: "Yes; wheresoever I will, I alight and set fire and do to death."

122. And I said to him: "By what angel art thou frustrated?" And he answered: "By the only-ruling God, that hath authority over me even to be heard. He that is to be born of a virgin and crucified by the Jews on a cross. Whom the angels and archangels worship. He doth frustrate me, and enfeeble me of my great strength, which has been given me by my father the devil." And I said to him: "What canst thou do?" And he answered: "I am able to remove mountains, to overthrow the oaths of kings. I wither trees and make their leaves to fall off."

And I said to him: "Canst thou raise this stone, and lay it for the beginning of this corner which exists in the fair plan of the Temple?" And he said: "Not only raise this, O king; but also, with the help of the demon who presides over the Red Sea, I will bring up the pillar of air, and will stand it where thou wilt in Jerusalem."

123. Saying this, I laid stress on him, and the flask became as if depleted of air. And I placed it under the stone, and (the spirit) girded himself up, and lifted it up top of the flask. And the flask went up the steps, carrying the stone, and laid it down at the end of the entrance of the Temple. And I Solomon, beholding the stone raised aloft and placed on a foundation, said: "Truly the Scripture is fulfilled, which says: 'The stone which the builders rejected on trial, that same is become the head of the corner.' For this it is not mine to grant, but God's, that the demon should be strong enough to lift up so great a stone and deposit it in the place I wished."

124. And Ephippas led the demon of the Red Sea with the column. And they both took the column and raised it aloft from the earth. And I outwitted these two spirits, so that they could not shake the entire earth in a moment of time. And then I sealed round with my [44] ring on this side and that, and said: "Watch."

And the spirits have remained upholding it until this day, for proof of the wisdom vouchsafed to me. And there the pillar was hanging of enormous size, in mid air, supported by the winds. And thus the spirits appeared underneath, like air, supporting it. And if one looks fixedly, the pillar is a little oblique, being supported by the spirits; and it is so to day.

125. And I Solomon questioned the other spirit which came up with the pillar from the depth of the

Red Sea. And I said to him: "Who art thou, and what calls thee? And what is thy business? For I hear many things about thee." And the demon answered: "I, O King Solomon, am called Abezithibod. I am a descendant of the archangel. Once as I sat in the first heaven, of which the name is Ameleouth -- I then am a fierce spirit and winged, and with a single wing, plotting against every spirit under heaven. I was present when Moses went in before Pharaoh, king of Egypt, and I hardened his heart. I am he whom Iannes and Iambres invoked homing with Moses in Egypt. I am he who fought against Moses with wonders with signs."

126. I said therefore to him: "How wast thou found in the Red Sea?" And he answered: "In the exodus of the sons of Israel I hardened the heart of Pharaoh. And I excited his heart and that of his ministers. And I caused them to pursue after the children of Israel. And Pharaoh followed with (me) and all the Egyptians.

Then I was present there, and we followed together. And we all came up upon the Red Sea. And it came to pass when the children of Israel had crossed over, the water returned and hid all the host of the Egyptians and all their might. And I remained in the sea, being kept under this pillar. But when Ephippas came, being sent by thee, shut up in the vessel of a flask, he fetched me up to thee."

127. I, therefore, Solomon, having heard this, glorified God and adjured the demons not to disobey me, but to remain supporting the pillar. And they both sware, saying: "The Lord thy God liveth, we will not let go this pillar until the world's end. But on whatever day this stone fall, then shall be the end of the world."

128. And I Solomon glorified God, and adorned the Temple of the Lord with all fair-seeming. And I was glad in spirit in my kingdom, and there was peace in my days. And I took wives of my own from every land, who were numberless. And I marched against the Jebusaeans, and there I saw Jebusaean, daughter of a man: and fell violently in love with her, and desired to take her to wife along with my other wives. And I said to their priests: "Give me the Sonmanites (i.e. Shunammite) to wife."

But the priests of Moloch said to me: "If thou lovest this maiden, go in and worship our gods, the great god Raphan and the god called Moloch." I therefore was in fear of the glory of God, and did not follow to worship. And I said to them: "I will not worship a strange god. What is this proposal, that ye compel me to do so much?" But they said: ". . . . . by our fathers."

129. And when I answered that I would on no account worship strange gods, they told the maiden not to sleep with me until I complied and sacrificed to the gods. I then was moved, but crafty Eros brought and laid by her for me five grasshoppers, saying: "Take these grasshoppers, and crush them together in the name of the god Moloch; and then will I sleep with you." And this I actually did. And at once the Spirit of God departed from me, and I became weak as well as foolish in my words. And after that I was obliged by her to build a temple of idols to Baal, and to Raphan, and to Moloch, and to the other idols.

130. I then, wretch that I am, followed her advice, and the glory of God quite departed from me; and my spirit was darkened, and I became the sport of idols and demons. Wherefore I wrote out this Testament, that ye who get possession of it may pity, and attend to the last things, and not to the first. So that ye may find grace for ever and ever.

Amen.

The Wisdom of Solomon

From the Books of the Apocrypha

Chapter One

1: Love righteousness, ye that be judges of the earth: think of the Lord with a good (heart,) and in simplicity of heart seek him.

2: For he will be found of them that tempt him not; and sheweth himself unto such as do not distrust him.

3: For forward thoughts separate from God: and his power, when it is tried, reproveth the unwise.

4: For into a malicious soul wisdom shall not enter; nor dwell in the body that is subject unto sin.

5: For the holy spirit of discipline will flee deceit, and remove from thoughts that are without understanding, and will not abide when unrighteousness cometh in.

6: For wisdom is a loving spirit; and will not acquit a blasphemer of his words: for God is witness of his reins, and a true beholder of his heart, and a hearer of his tongue.

7: For the Spirit of the Lord filleth the world: and that which containeth all things hath knowledge of the voice.

8: Therefore he that speaketh unrighteous things cannot be hid: neither shall vengeance, when it punisheth, pass by him.

9: For inquisition shall be made into the counsels of the ungodly: and the sound of his words shall come unto the Lord for the manifestation of his wicked deeds.

10: For the ear of jealousy heareth all things: and the noise of murmurings is not hid.

11: Therefore beware of murmuring, which is unprofitable; and refrain your tongue from backbiting: for there is no word so secret, that shall go for nought: and the mouth that belieth slayeth the soul.

12: Seek not death in the error of your life: and pull not upon yourselves destruction with the works of your hands.

13: For God made not death: neither hath he pleasure in the destruction of the living.

14: For he created all things, that they might have their being: and the generations of the world were healthful; and there is no poison of destruction in them, nor the kingdom of death upon the earth:

15: (For righteousness is immortal:)

16: But ungodly men with their works and words called it to them: for when they thought to have it their friend, they consumed to nought, and made a covenant with it, because they are worthy to take part with it.

Chapter Two

1: For the ungodly said, reasoning with themselves, but not aright, Our life is short and tedious, and in the death of a man there is no remedy: neither was there any man known to have returned from the grave.

2: For we are born at all adventure: and we shall be hereafter as though we had never been: for the breath in our nostrils is as smoke, and a little spark in the moving of our heart:

3: Which being extinguished, our body shall be turned into ashes, and our spirit shall vanish as the soft air,

4: And our name shall be forgotten in time, and no man shall have our works in remembrance, and our life shall pass away as the trace of a cloud, and shall be dispersed as a mist, that is driven away with the beams of the sun, and overcome with the heat thereof.

5: For our time is a very shadow that passeth away; and after our end there is no returning: for it is fast sealed, so that no man cometh again.

6: Come on therefore, let us enjoy the good things

that are present: and let us speedily use the creatures like as in youth.

7: Let us fill ourselves with costly wine and ointments: and let no flower of the spring pass by us:

8: Let us crown ourselves with rosebuds, before they be withered:

9: Let none of us go without his part of our voluptuousness: let us leave tokens of our joyfulness in every place: for this is our portion, and our lot is this.

10: Let us oppress the poor righteous man, let us not spare the widow, nor reverence the ancient gray hairs of the aged.

11: Let our strength be the law of justice: for that which is feeble is found to be nothing worth.
12: Therefore let us lie in wait for the righteous; because he is not for our turn, and he is clean contrary to our doings: he upbraideth us with our offending the law, and objecteth to our infamy the transgressings of our education.

13: He professeth to have the knowledge of God: and he calleth himself the child of the Lord.

14: He was made to reprove our thoughts.

15: He is grievous unto us even to behold: for his life is not like other men's, his ways are of another fashion.

16: We are esteemed of him as counterfeits: he abstaineth from our ways as from filthiness: he pronounceth the end of the just to be blessed, and maketh his boast that God is his father.

17: Let us see if his words be true: and let us prove what shall happen in the end of him.

18: For if the just man be the son of God, he will help him, and deliver him from the hand of his enemies.

19: Let us examine him with despitefulness and torture, that we may know his meekness, and prove his patience.

20: Let us condemn him with a shameful death: for by his own saying he shall be respected.

21: Such things they did imagine, and were deceived: for their own wickedness hath blinded them.

22: As for the mysteries of God, they knew them not: neither hoped they for the wages of righteousness, nor discerned a reward for blameless souls.

23: For God created man to be immortal, and made him to be an image of his own eternity.

24: Nevertheless through envy of the devil came death into the world: and they that do hold of his side do find it.

Chapter Three

1: But the souls of the righteous are in the hand of God, and there shall no torment touch them.

2: In the sight of the unwise they seemed to die: and their departure is taken for misery,

3: And their going from us to be utter destruction: but they are in peace.

4: For though they be punished in the sight of men, yet is their hope full of immortality.

5: And having been a little chastised, they shall be greatly rewarded: for God proved them, and found them worthy for himself.

6: As gold in the furnace hath he tried them, and received them as a burnt offering.

7: And in the time of their visitation they shall shine, and run to and fro like sparks among the stubble.

8: They shall judge the nations, and have dominion over the people, and their Lord shall reign for ever.

9: They that put their trust in him shall understand

the truth: and such as be faithful in love shall abide with him: for grace and mercy is to his saints, and he hath care for his elect.

10: But the ungodly shall be punished according to their own imaginations, which have neglected the righteous, and forsaken the Lord.

11: For whoso despiseth wisdom and nurture, he is miserable, and their hope is vain, their labours unfruitful, and their works unprofitable:

12: Their wives are foolish, and their children wicked:

13: Their offspring is cursed. Wherefore blessed is the barren that is undefiled, which hath not known the sinful bed: she shall have fruit in the visitation of souls.

14: And blessed is the eunuch, which with his hands hath wrought no iniquity, nor imagined wicked things against God: for unto him shall be given the special gift of faith, and an inheritance in the temple of the Lord more acceptable to his mind.

15: For glorious is the fruit of good labours: and the root of wisdom shall never fall away.

16: As for the children of adulterers, they shall not come to their perfection, and the seed of an unrighteous bed shall be rooted out.

17: For though they live long, yet shall they be nothing regarded: and their last age shall be without honour.

18: Or, if they die quickly, they have no hope, neither comfort in the day of trial.

19: For horrible is the end of the unrighteous generation.

Chapter Four

1: Better it is to have no children, and to have virtue: for the memorial thereof is immortal: because it is known with God, and with men.

2: When it is present, men take example at it; and when it is gone, they desire it: it weareth a crown, and triumpheth for ever, having gotten the victory, striving for undefiled rewards.

3: But the multiplying brood of the ungodly shall not thrive, nor take deep rooting from bastard slips, nor lay any fast foundation.

4: For though they flourish in branches for a time; yet standing not last, they shall be shaken with the wind, and through the force of winds they shall be rooted out.

5: The imperfect branches shall be broken off, their fruit unprofitable, not ripe to eat, yea, meet for nothing.

6: For children begotten of unlawful beds are witnesses of wickedness against their parents in their trial.

7: But though the righteous be prevented with death, yet shall he be in rest.

8: For honourable age is not that which standeth in length of time, nor that is measured by number of years.

9: But wisdom is the gray hair unto men, and an unspotted life is old age.

10: He pleased God, and was beloved of him: so that living among sinners he was translated.

11: Yea speedily was he taken away, lest that wickedness should alter his understanding, or deceit beguile his soul.

12: For the bewitching of naughtiness doth obscure things that are honest; and the wandering of concupiscence doth undermine the simple mind.

13: He, being made perfect in a short time, fulfilled a long time:

14: For his soul pleased the Lord: therefore hasted he to take him away from among the wicked.

15: This the people saw, and understood it not, neither laid they up this in their minds, That his grace and mercy is with his saints, and that he hath respect unto his chosen.

16: Thus the righteous that is dead shall condemn the ungodly which are living; and youth that is soon perfected the many years and old age of the unrighteous.

17: For they shall see the end of the wise, and shall not understand what God in his counsel hath decreed of him, and to what end the Lord hath set him in safety.

18: They shall see him, and despise him; but God shall laugh them to scorn: and they shall hereafter be a vile carcase, and a reproach among the dead for evermore.

19: For he shall rend them, and cast them down headlong, that they shall be speechless; and he shall shake them from the foundation; and they shall be utterly laid waste, and be in sorrow; and their memorial shall perish.

20: And when they cast up the accounts of their sins, they shall come with fear: and their own iniquities shall convince them to their face.

Chapter Five

1: Then shall the righteous man stand in great boldness before the face of such as have afflicted him, and made no account of his labours.

2: When they see it, they shall be troubled with terrible fear, and shall be amazed at the strangeness of his salvation, so far beyond all that they looked for.

3: And they repenting and groaning for anguish of spirit shall say within themselves, This was he, whom we had sometimes in derision, and a proverb of reproach:

4: We fools accounted his life madness, and his end to be without honour:

5: How is he numbered among the children of God, and his lot is among the saints!

6: Therefore have we erred from the way of truth, and the light of righteousness hath not shined unto us, and the sun of righteousness rose not upon us.

7: We wearied ourselves in the way of wickedness and destruction: yea, we have gone through deserts, where there lay no way: but as for the way of the Lord, we have not known it.

8: What hath pride profited us? or what good hath riches with our vaunting brought us?

9: All those things are passed away like a shadow, and as a post that hasted by;
10: And as a ship that passeth over the waves of the water, which when it is gone by, the trace thereof cannot be found, neither the pathway of the keel in the waves;

11: Or as when a bird hath flown through the air, there is no token of her way to be found, but the light air being beaten with the stroke of her wings and parted with the violent noise and motion of them, is passed through, and therein afterwards no sign where she went is to be found;

12: Or like as when an arrow is shot at a mark, it parteth the air, which immediately cometh together again, so that a man cannot know where it went through:

13: Even so we in like manner, as soon as we were born, began to draw to our end, and had no sign of virtue to shew; but were consumed in our own wickedness.

14: For the hope of the ungodly is like dust that is blown away with the wind; like a thin froth that is driven away with the storm; like as the smoke which is dispersed here and there with a tempest, and passeth away as the remembrance of a guest that tarrieth but a day.

15: But the righteous live for evermore; their reward also is with the Lord, and the care of them is with the most High.

16: Therefore shall they receive a glorious kingdom, and a beautiful crown from the Lord's hand: for with his right hand shall he cover them, and with his arm shall he protect them.

17: He shall take to him his jealousy for complete armour, and make the creature his weapon for the revenge of his enemies.

18: He shall put on righteousness as a breastplate, and true judgment instead of an helmet.

19: He shall take holiness for an invincible shield.

20: His severe wrath shall he sharpen for a sword, and the world shall fight with him against the unwise.

21: Then shall the right aiming thunderbolts go abroad; and from the clouds, as from a well drawn bow, shall they fly to the mark.

22: And hailstones full of wrath shall be cast as out of a stone bow, and the water of the sea shall rage against them, and the floods shall cruelly drown them.

23: Yea, a mighty wind shall stand up against them, and like a storm shall blow them away: thus iniquity shall lay waste the whole earth, and ill dealing shall overthrow the thrones of the mighty.

Chapter Six

1: Hear therefore, O ye kings, and understand; learn, ye that be judges of the ends of the earth.

2: Give ear, ye that rule the people, and glory in the multitude of nations.

3: For power is given you of the Lord, and sovereignty from the Highest, who shall try your works, and search out your counsels.

4: Because, being ministers of his kingdom, ye have not judged aright, nor kept the law, nor walked after the counsel of God;

5: Horribly and speedily shall he come upon you: for a sharp judgment shall be to them that be in high places.

6: For mercy will soon pardon the meanest: but mighty men shall be mightily tormented.

7: For he which is Lord over all shall fear no man's person, neither shall he stand in awe of any man's greatness: for he hath made the small and great, and careth for all alike.

8: But a sore trial shall come upon the mighty.

9: Unto you therefore, O kings, do I speak, that ye may learn wisdom, and not fall away.

10: For they that keep holiness holily shall be judged

holy: and they that have learned such things shall find what to answer.

11: Wherefore set your affection upon my words; desire them, and ye shall be instructed.
12: Wisdom is glorious, and never fadeth away: yea, she is easily seen of them that love her, and found of such as seek her.

13: She preventeth them that desire her, in making herself first known unto them.

14: Whoso seeketh her early shall have no great travail: for he shall find her sitting at his doors.

15: To think therefore upon her is perfection of wisdom: and whoso watcheth for her shall quickly be without care.

16: For she goeth about seeking such as are worthy of her, sheweth herself favourably unto them in the ways, and meeteth them in every thought.

17: For the very true beginning of her is the desire of discipline; and the care of discipline is love;

18: And love is the keeping of her laws; and the

giving heed unto her laws is the assurance of incorruption;

19: And incorruption maketh us near unto God:

20: Therefore the desire of wisdom bringeth to a kingdom.

21: If your delight be then in thrones and sceptres, O ye kings of the people, honour wisdom, that ye may reign for evermore.

22: As for wisdom, what she is, and how she came up, I will tell you, and will not hide mysteries from you: but will seek her out from the beginning of her nativity, and bring the knowledge of her into light, and will not pass over the truth.

23: Neither will I go with consuming envy; for such a man shall have no fellowship with wisdom.

24: But the multitude of the wise is the welfare of the world: and a wise king is the upholding of the people.

25: Receive therefore instruction through my words, and it shall do you good.

Chapter Seven

1: I myself also am a mortal man, like to all, and the offspring of him that was first made of the earth,

2: And in my mother's womb was fashioned to be flesh in the time of ten months, being compacted in blood, of the seed of man, and the pleasure that came with sleep.

3: And when I was born, I drew in the common air, and fell upon the earth, which is of like nature, and the first voice which I uttered was crying, as all others do.

4: I was nursed in swaddling clothes, and that with cares.

5: For there is no king that had any other beginning of birth.

6: For all men have one entrance into life, and the like going out.

7: Wherefore I prayed, and understanding was given

me: I called upon God, and the spirit of wisdom came to me.

8: I preferred her before sceptres and thrones, and esteemed riches nothing in comparison of her.

9: Neither compared I unto her any precious stone, because all gold in respect of her is as a little sand, and silver shall be counted as clay before her.

10: I loved her above health and beauty, and chose to have her instead of light: for the light that cometh from her never goeth out.

11: All good things together came to me with her, and innumerable riches in her hands.
12: And I rejoiced in them all, because wisdom goeth before them: and I knew not that she was the mother of them.

13: I learned diligently, and do communicate her liberally: I do not hide her riches.

14: For she is a treasure unto men that never faileth: which they that use become the friends of God, being commended for the gifts that come from learning.

15: God hath granted me to speak as I would, and to conceive as is meet for the things that are given me: because it is he that leadeth unto wisdom, and directeth the wise.

16: For in his hand are both we and our words; all wisdom also, and knowledge of workmanship.

17: For he hath given me certain knowledge of the things that are, namely, to know how the world was made, and the operation of the elements:

18: The beginning, ending, and midst of the times: the alterations of the turning of the sun, and the change of seasons:

19: The circuits of years, and the positions of stars:

20: The natures of living creatures, and the furies of wild beasts: the violence of winds, and the reasonings of men: the diversities of plants and the virtues of roots:

21: And all such things as are either secret or manifest, them I know.

22: For wisdom, which is the worker of all things, taught me: for in her is an understanding spirit holy, one only, manifold, subtil, lively, clear, undefiled, plain, not subject to hurt, loving the thing that is good quick, which cannot be letted, ready to do good,

23: Kind to man, steadfast, sure, free from care, having all power, overseeing all things, and going through all understanding, pure, and most subtil, spirits.

24: For wisdom is more moving than any motion: she passeth and goeth through all things by reason of her pureness.

25: For she is the breath of the power of God, and a pure influence flowing from the glory of the Almighty: therefore can no defiled thing fall into her.

26: For she is the brightness of the everlasting light, the unspotted mirror of the power of God, and the image of his goodness.

27: And being but one, she can do all things: and remaining in herself, she maketh all things new: and in all ages entering into holy souls, she maketh them friends of God, and prophets.

28: For God loveth none but him that dwelleth with wisdom.

29: For she is more beautiful than the sun, and above all the order of stars: being compared with the light, she is found before it.

30: For after this cometh night: but vice shall not prevail against wisdom.

Chapter Eight

1: Wisdom reacheth from one end to another mightily: and sweetly doth she order all things.

2: I loved her, and sought her out from my youth, I desired to make her my spouse, and I was a lover of her beauty.

3: In that she is conversant with God, she magnifieth her nobility: yea, the Lord of all things himself loved her.

4: For she is privy to the mysteries of the knowledge of God, and a lover of his works.

5: If riches be a possession to be desired in this life; what is richer than wisdom, that worketh all things?

6: And if prudence work; who of all that are is a more cunning workman than she?

7: And if a man love righteousness her labours are virtues: for she teacheth temperance and prudence, justice and fortitude: which are such things, as en can have nothing more profitable in their life.

8: If a man desire much experience, she knoweth things of old, and conjectureth aright what is to come: she knoweth the subtilties of speeches, and can expound dark sentences: she foreseeth signs and wonders, and the events of seasons and times.

9: Therefore I purposed to take her to me to live with me, knowing that she would be a counsellor of good things, and a comfort in cares and grief.

10: For her sake I shall have estimation among the multitude, and honour with the elders, though I be young.

11: I shall be found of a quick conceit in judgment, and shall be admired in the sight of great men.

12: When I hold my tongue, they shall bide my leisure, and when I speak, they shall give good ear unto me: if I talk much, they shall lay their hands upon their mouth.

13: Moreover by the means of her I shall obtain immortality, and leave behind me an everlasting memorial to them that come after me.
14: I shall set the people in order, and the nations shall be subject unto me.

15: Horrible tyrants shall be afraid, when they do but hear of me; I shall be found good among the multitude, and valiant in war.

16: After I am come into mine house, I will repose myself with her: for her conversation hath no bitterness; and to live with her hath no sorrow, but mirth and joy.

17: Now when I considered these things in myself, and pondered them in my heart, how that to be allied unto wisdom is immortality;

18: And great pleasure it is to have her friendship; and in the works of her hands are infinite riches; and in the exercise of conference with her, prudence; and in talking with her, a good report; I went about seeking how to take her to me.

19: For I was a witty child, and had a good spirit.
20: Yea rather, being good, I came into a body undefiled.

21: Nevertheless, when I perceived that I could not otherwise obtain her, except God gave her me; and that was a point of wisdom also to know whose gift she was; I prayed unto the Lord, and besought him, and with my whole heart I said,

Chapter Nine

1: O God of my fathers, and Lord of mercy, who hast made all things with thy word,

2: And ordained man through thy wisdom, that he should have dominion over the creatures which thou hast made,

3: And order the world according to equity and righteousness, and execute judgment with an upright heart:

4: Give me wisdom, that sitteth by thy throne; and reject me not from among thy children:

5: For I thy servant and son of thine handmaid am a feeble person, and of a short time, and too young for the understanding of judgment and laws.

6: For though a man be never so perfect among the

children of men, yet if thy wisdom be not with him, he shall be nothing regarded.

7: Thou hast chosen me to be a king of thy people, and a judge of thy sons and daughters:

8: Thou hast commanded me to build a temple upon thy holy mount, and an altar in the city wherein thou dwellest, a resemblance of the holy tabernacle, which thou hast prepared from the beginning.

9: And wisdom was with thee: which knoweth thy works, and was present when thou madest the world, and knew what was acceptable in thy sight, and right in thy commandments.

10: O send her out of thy holy heavens, and from the throne of thy glory, that being present she may labour with me, that I may know what is pleasing unto thee.

11: For she knoweth and understandeth all things, and she shall lead me soberly in my doings, and preserve me in her power.

12: So shall my works be acceptable, and then shall I judge thy people righteously, and be worthy to sit in my father's seat.

13: For what man is he that can know the counsel of God? or who can think what the will of the Lord is?

14: For the thoughts of mortal men are miserable, and our devices are but uncertain.

15: For the corruptible body presseth down the soul, and the earthy tabernacle weigheth down the mind that museth upon many things.

16: And hardly do we guess aright at things that are upon earth, and with labour do we find the things that are before us: but the things that are in heaven who hath searched out?

17: And thy counsel who hath known, except thou give wisdom, and send thy Holy Spirit from above?

18: For so the ways of them which lived on the earth were reformed, and men were taught the things that are pleasing unto thee, and were saved through wisdom.

Chapter Ten

1: She preserved the first formed father of the world, that was created alone, and brought him out of his fall,

2: And gave him power to rule all things.

3: But when the unrighteous went away from her in his anger, he perished also in the fury wherewith he murdered his brother.

4: For whose cause the earth being drowned with the flood, wisdom again preserved it, and directed the course of the righteous in a piece of wood of small value.

5: Moreover, the nations in their wicked conspiracy being confounded, she found out the righteous, and preserved him blameless unto God, and kept him strong against his tender compassion toward his son.

6: When the ungodly perished, she delivered the righteous man, who fled from the fire which fell down upon the five cities.

7: Of whose wickedness even to this day the waste land that smoketh is a testimony, and plants bearing fruit that never come to ripeness: and a standing pillar of salt is a monument of an unbelieving soul.

8: For regarding not wisdom, they gat not only this hurt, that they knew not the things which were good; but also left behind them to the world a memorial of their foolishness: so that in the things wherein they offended they could not so much as be hid.

9: Rut wisdom delivered from pain those that attended upon her.

10: When the righteous fled from his brother's wrath she guided him in right paths, shewed him the kingdom of God, and gave him knowledge of holy things, made him rich in his travels, and multiplied the fruit of his labours.

11: In the covetousness of such as oppressed him she stood by him, and made him rich.

12: She defended him from his enemies, and kept him safe from those that lay in wait, and in a sore conflict she gave him the victory; that he might know that goodness is stronger than all.

13: When the righteous was sold, she forsook him

not, but delivered him from sin: she went down with him into the pit,

14: And left him not in bonds, till she brought him the sceptre of the kingdom, and power against those that oppressed him: as for them that had accused him, she shewed them to be liars, and gave him perpetual glory.

15: She delivered the righteous people and blameless seed from the nation that oppressed them.

16: She entered into the soul of the servant of the Lord, and withstood dreadful kings in wonders and signs;

17: Rendered to the righteous a reward of their labours, guided them in a marvellous way, and was unto them for a cover by day, and a light of stars in the night season;

18: Brought them through the Red sea, and led them through much water:

19: But she drowned their enemies, and cast them up out of the bottom of the deep.

20: Therefore the righteous spoiled the ungodly, and

praised thy holy name, O Lord, and magnified with one accord thine hand, that fought for them.

21: For wisdom opened the mouth of the dumb, and made the tongues of them that cannot speak eloquent.

Chapter Eleven

1: She prospered their works in the hand of the holy prophet.

2: They went through the wilderness that was not inhabited, and pitched tents in places where there lay no way.

3: They stood against their enemies, and were avenged of their adversaries.

4: When they were thirsty, they called upon thee, and water was given the

m out of the flinty rock, and their thirst was quenched out of the hard stone.

5: For by what things their enemies were punished, by the same they in their need were benefited.

6: For instead of of a perpetual running river troubled with foul blood,

7: For a manifest reproof of that commandment, whereby the infants were slain, thou gavest unto them abundance of water by a means which they hoped not for:

8: Declaring by that thirst then how thou hadst punished their adversaries.

9: For when they were tried albeit but in mercy chastised, they knew how the ungodly were judged in wrath and tormented, thirsting in another manner than the just.

10: For these thou didst admonish and try, as a father: but the other, as a severe king, thou didst condemn and punish.

11: Whether they were absent or present, they were vexed alike.
12: For a double grief came upon them, and a groaning for the remembrance of things past.

13: For when they heard by their own punishments

the other to be benefited, they had some feeling of the Lord.

14: For whom they respected with scorn, when he was long before thrown out at the casting forth of the infants, him in the end, when they saw what came to pass, they admired.

15: But for the foolish devices of their wickedness, wherewith being deceived they worshipped serpents void of reason, and vile beasts, thou didst send a multitude of unreasonable beasts upon them for vengeance;

16: That they might know, that wherewithal a man sinneth, by the same also shall he be punished.

17: For thy Almighty hand, that made the world of matter without form, wanted not means to send among them a multitude of bears or fierce lions,

18: Or unknown wild beasts, full of rage, newly created, breathing out either a fiery vapour, or filthy scents of scattered smoke, or shooting horrible sparkles out of their eyes:

19: Whereof not only the harm might dispatch them

at once, but also the terrible sight utterly destroy them.

20: Yea, and without these might they have fallen down with one blast, being persecuted of vengeance, and scattered abroad through the breath of thy power: but thou hast ordered all things in measure and number and weight.

21: For thou canst shew thy great strength at all times when thou wilt; and who may withstand the power of thine arm?

22: For the whole world before thee is as a little grain of the balance, yea, as a drop of the morning dew that falleth down upon the earth.

23: But thou hast mercy upon all; for thou canst do all things, and winkest at the sins of men, because they should amend.

24: For thou lovest all the things that are, and abhorrest nothing which thou hast made: for never wouldest thou have made any thing, if thou hadst hated it.

25: And how could any thing have endured, if it had

not been thy will? or been preserved, if not called by thee?

26: But thou sparest all: for they are thine, O Lord, thou lover of souls.

Chapter Twelve

1: For thine incorruptible Spirit is in all things.

2: Therefore chastenest thou them by little and little that offend, and warnest them by putting them in remembrance wherein they have offended, that leaving their wickedness they may believe on thee, O Lord.

3: For it was thy will to destroy by the hands of our fathers both those old inhabitants of thy holy land,

4: Whom thou hatedst for doing most odious works of witchcrafts, and wicked sacrifices;

5: And also those merciless murderers of children, and devourers of man's flesh, and the feasts of blood,

6: With their priests out of the midst of their idolatrous crew, and the parents, that killed with their own hands souls destitute of help:

7: That the land, which thou esteemedst above all other, might receive a worthy colony of God's children.

8: Nevertheless even those thou sparedst as men, and didst send wasps, forerunners of thine host, to destroy them by little and little.

9: Not that thou wast unable to bring the ungodly under the hand of the righteous in battle, or to destroy them at once with cruel beasts, or with one rough word:

10: But executing thy judgments upon them by little and little, thou gavest them place of repentance, not being ignorant that they were a naughty generation, and that their malice was bred in them, and that their cogitation would never be changed.

11: For it was a cursed seed from the beginning; neither didst thou for fear of any man give them pardon for those things wherein they sinned.

12: For who shall say, What hast thou done? or who shall withstand thy judgment? or who shall accuse thee for the nations that perish, whom thou made? or who shall come to stand against thee, to be revenged for the unrighteous men?

13: For neither is there any God but thou that careth for all, to whom thou mightest shew that thy judgment is not unright.

14: Neither shall king or tyrant be able to set his face against thee for any whom thou hast punished.

15: Forsomuch then as thou art righteous thyself, thou orderest all things righteously: thinking it not agreeable with thy power to condemn him that hath not deserved to be punished.

16: For thy power is the beginning of righteousness, and because thou art the Lord of all, it maketh thee to be gracious unto all.

17: For when men will not believe that thou art of a full power, thou shewest thy strength, and among them that know it thou makest their boldness manifest.

18: But thou, mastering thy power, judgest with equity, and orderest us with great favour: for thou mayest use power when thou wilt.

19: But by such works hast thou taught thy people that the just man should be merciful, and hast made thy children to be of a good hope that thou givest repentance for sins.

20: For if thou didst punish the enemies of thy children, and the condemned to death, with such deliberation, giving them time and place, whereby they might be delivered from their malice:

21: With how great circumspection didst thou judge thine own sons, unto whose fathers thou hast sworn, and made covenants of good promises?

22: Therefore, whereas thou dost chasten us, thou scourgest our enemies a thousand times more, to the intent that, when we judge, we should carefully think of thy goodness, and when we ourselves are judged, we should look for mercy.

23: Wherefore, whereas men have lived dissolutely and unrighteously, thou hast tormented them with their own abominations.

24: For they went astray very far in the ways of error, and held them for gods, which even among the beasts of their enemies were despised, being deceived, as children of no understanding.

25: Therefore unto them, as to children without the

use of reason, thou didst send a judgment to mock them.

26: But they that would not be reformed by that correction, wherein he dallied with them, shall feel a judgment worthy of God.

27: For, look, for what things they grudged, when they were punished, that is, for them whom they thought to be gods; [now] being punished in them, when they saw it, they acknowledged him to be the true God, whom before they denied to know: and therefore came extreme damnation upon them.

Chapter Thirteen

1: Surely vain are all men by nature, who are ignorant of God, and could not out of the good things that are seen know him that is: neither by considering the works did they acknowledge the workmaster;

2: But deemed either fire, or wind, or the swift air, or the circle of the stars, or the violent water, or the lights of heaven, to be the gods which govern the world.

3: With whose beauty if they being delighted took them to be gods; let them know how much better the Lord of them is: for the first author of beauty hath created them.

4: But if they were astonished at their power and virtue, let them understand by them, how much mightier he is that made them.

5: For by the greatness and beauty of the creatures proportionably the maker of them is seen.

6: But yet for this they are the less to be blamed: for they peradventure err, seeking God, and desirous to find him.

7: For being conversant in his works they search him diligently, and believe their sight: because the things are beautiful that are seen.

8: Howbeit neither are they to be pardoned.

9: For if they were able to know so much, that they could aim at the world; how did they not sooner find out the Lord thereof?

10: But miserable are they, and in dead things is their hope, who call them gods, which are the works of men's hands, gold and silver, to shew art in, and resemblances of beasts, or a stone good for nothing, the work of an ancient hand.

11: Now a carpenter that felleth timber, after he hath sawn down a tree meet for the purpose, and taken off all the bark skillfully round about, and hath wrought it handsomely, and made a vessel thereof fit for the service of man's life;

12: And after spending the refuse of his work to dress his meat, hath filled himself;

13: And taking the very refuse among those which served to no use, being a crooked piece of wood, and full of knots, hath carved it diligently, when he had nothing else to do, and formed it by the skill of his understanding, and fashioned it to the image of a man;

14: Or made it like some vile beast, laying it over with vermilion, and with paint colouring it red, and covering every spot therein;

15: And when he had made a convenient room for it, set it in a wall, and made it fast with iron:

16: For he provided for it that it might not fall,

knowing that it was unable to help itself; for it is an image, and hath need of help:

17: Then maketh he prayer for his goods, for his wife and children, and is not ashamed to speak to that which hath no life.

18: For health he calleth upon that which is weak: for life prayeth to that which is dead; for aid humbly beseecheth that which hath least means to help: and for a good journey he asketh of that which cannot set a foot forward:

19: And for gaining and getting, and for good success of his hands, asketh ability to do of him, that is most unable to do any thing.

Chapter Fourteen

1: Again, one preparing himself to sail, and about to pass through the raging waves, calleth upon a piece of wood more rotten than the vessel that carrieth him.

2: For verily desire of gain devised that, and the workman built it by his skill.

3: But thy providence, O Father, governeth it: for thou hast made a way in the sea, and a safe path in the waves;

4: Shewing that thou canst save from all danger: yea, though a man went to sea without art.

5: Nevertheless thou wouldest not that the works of thy wisdom should be idle, and therefore do men commit their lives to a small piece of wood, and passing the rough sea in a weak vessel are saved.

6: For in the old time also, when the proud giants perished, the hope of the world governed by thy hand escaped in a weak vessel, and left to all ages a seed of generation.

7: For blessed is the wood whereby righteousness cometh.

8: But that which is made with hands is cursed, as well it, as he that made it: he, because he made it; and it, because, being corruptible, it was called god.

9: For the ungodly and his ungodliness are both alike hateful unto God.

10: For that which is made shall be punished together with him that made it.

11: Therefore even upon the idols of the Gentiles shall there be a visitation: because in the creature of God they are become an abomination, and stumblingblocks to the souls of men, and a snare to the feet of the unwise.

12: For the devising of idols was the beginning of spiritual fornication, and the invention of them the corruption of life.

13: For neither were they from the beginning, neither shall they be for ever.

14: For by the vain glory of men they entered into the world, and therefore shall they come shortly to an end.

15: For a father afflicted with untimely mourning, when he hath made an image of his child soon taken away, now honoured him as a god, which was then a dead man, and delivered to those that were under him ceremonies and sacrifices.

16: Thus in process of time an ungodly custom grown strong was kept as a law, and graven images were worshipped by the commandments of kings.

17: Whom men could not honour in presence, because they dwelt far off, they took the counterfeit of his visage from far, and made an express image of a king whom they honoured, to the end that by this their forwardness they might flatter him that was absent, as if he were present.

18: Also the singular diligence of the artificer did help to set forward the ignorant to more superstition.

19: For he, peradventure willing to please one in authority, forced all his skill to make the resemblance of the best fashion.

20: And so the multitude, allured by the grace of the work, took him now for a god, which a little before was but honoured.

21: And this was an occasion to deceive the world: for men, serving either calamity or tyranny, did ascribe unto stones and stocks the incommunicable name.

22: Moreover this was not enough for them, that they erred in the knowledge of God; but whereas they lived in the great war of ignorance, those so great plagues called they peace.

23: For whilst they slew their children in sacrifices, or used secret ceremonies, or made revellings of strange rites;

24: They kept neither lives nor marriages any longer undefiled: but either one slew another traiterously, or grieved him by adultery.

25: So that there reigned in all men without exception blood, manslaughter, theft, and dissimulation, corruption, unfaithfulness, tumults, perjury,

26: Disquieting of good men, forgetfulness of good turns, defiling of souls, changing of kind, disorder in marriages, adultery, and shameless uncleanness.

27: For the worshipping of idols not to be named is the beginning, the cause, and the end, of all evil.

28: For either they are mad when they be merry, or prophesy lies, or live unjustly, or else lightly forswear themselves.

29: For insomuch as their trust is in idols, which have no life; though they swear falsely, yet they look not to be hurt.

30: Howbeit for both causes shall they be justly punished: both because they thought not well of God, giving heed unto idols, and also unjustly swore in deceit, despising holiness.

31: For it is not the power of them by whom they swear: but it is the just vengeance of sinners, that punisheth always the offence of the ungodly.

Chapter Fifteen

1: But thou, O God, art gracious and true, longsuffering, and in mercy ordering all things,

2: For if we sin, we are thine, knowing thy power: but we will not sin, knowing that we are counted thine.

3: For to know thee is perfect righteousness: yea, to know thy power is the root of immortality.

4: For neither did the mischievous invention of men deceive us, nor an image spotted with divers colours, the painter's fruitless labour;

5: The sight whereof enticeth fools to lust after it, and so they desire the form of a dead image, that hath no breath.

6: Both they that make them, they that desire them, and they that worship them, are lovers of evil things, and are worthy to have such things to trust upon.

7: For the potter, tempering soft earth, fashioneth every vessel with much labour for our service: yea, of the same clay he maketh both the vessels that serve for clean uses, and likewise also all such as serve to the contrary: but what is the use of either sort, the potter himself is the judge.

8: And employing his labours lewdly, he maketh a vain god of the same clay, even he which a little before was made of earth himself, and within a little while after returneth to the same, out when his life which was lent him shall be demanded.

9: Notwithstanding his care is, not that he shall have much labour, nor that his life is short: but striveth to excel goldsmiths and silversmiths, and endeavoureth to do like the workers in brass, and counteth it his glory to make counterfeit things.

10: His heart is ashes, his hope is more vile than earth, and his life of less value than clay:

11: Forasmuch as he knew not his Maker, and him that inspired into him an active soul, and breathed in a living spirit.

12: But they counted our life a pastime, and our time here a market for gain: for, say they, we must be getting every way, though it be by evil means.

13: For this man, that of earthly matter maketh brittle vessels and graven images, knoweth himself to offend above all others.

14: And all the enemies of thy people, that hold them in subjection, are most foolish, and are more miserable than very babes.

15: For they counted all the idols of the heathen to be gods: which neither have the use of eyes to see, nor noses to draw breath, nor ears to hear, nor fingers of hands to handle; and as for their feet, they are slow to go.

16: For man made them, and he that borrowed his

own spirit fashioned them: but no man can make a god like unto himself.

17: For being mortal, he worketh a dead thing with wicked hands: for he himself is better than the things which he worshippeth: whereas he lived once, but they never.

18: Yea, they worshipped those beasts also that are most hateful: for being compared together, some are worse than others.

19: Neither are they beautiful, so much as to be desired in respect of beasts: but they went without the praise of God and his blessing.

Chapter Sixteen

1: Therefore by the like were they punished worthily, and by the multitude of beasts tormented.

2: Instead of which punishment, dealing graciously with thine own people, thou preparedst for them meat of a strange taste, even quails to stir up their appetite:

3: To the end that they, desiring food, might for the ugly sight of the beasts sent among them lothe even that, which they must needs desire; but these, suffering penury for a short space, might be made partakers of a strange taste.

4: For it was requisite, that upon them exercising tyranny should come penury, which they could not avoid: but to these it should only be shewed how their enemies were tormented.

5: For when the horrible fierceness of beasts came upon these, and they perished with the stings of crooked serpents, thy wrath endured not for ever:

6: But they were troubled for a small season, that they might be admonished, having a sign of salvation, to put them in remembrance of the commandment of thy law.

7: For he that turned himself toward it was not saved by the thing that he saw, but by thee, that art the Saviour of all.

8: And in this thou madest thine enemies confess, that it is thou who deliverest from all evil:

9: For them the bitings of grasshoppers and flies

killed, neither was there found any remedy for their life: for they were worthy to be punished by such.

10: But thy sons not the very teeth of venomous dragons overcame: for thy mercy was ever by them, and healed them.

11: For they were pricked, that they should remember thy words; and were quickly saved, that not falling into deep forgetfulness, they might be continually mindful of thy goodness.

12: For it was neither herb, nor mollifying plaister, that restored them to health: but thy word, O Lord, which healeth all things.

13: For thou hast power of life and death: thou leadest to the gates of hell, and bringest up again.

14: A man indeed killeth through his malice: and the spirit, when it is gone forth, returneth not; neither the soul received up cometh again.

15: But it is not possible to escape thine hand.

16: For the ungodly, that denied to know thee, were scourged by the strength of thine arm: with strange rains, hails, and showers, were they persecuted, that they could not avoid, and through fire were they consumed.

17: For, which is most to be wondered at, the fire had more force in the water, that quencheth all things: for the world fighteth for the righteous.

18: For sometime the flame was mitigated, that it might not burn up the beasts that were sent against the ungodly; but themselves might see and perceive that they were persecuted with the judgment of God.

19: And at another time it burneth even in the midst of water above the power of fire, that it might destroy the fruits of an unjust land.

20: Instead whereof thou feddest thine own people with angels' food, and didst send them from heaven bread prepared without their labour, able to content every man's delight, and agreeing to every taste.

21: For thy sustenance declared thy sweetness unto thy children, and serving to the appetite of the eater, tempered itself to every man's liking.

22: But snow and ice endured the fire, and melted not, that they might know that fire burning in the hail, and sparkling in the rain, did destroy the fruits of the enemies.

23: But this again did even forget his own strength, that the righteous might be nourished.

24: For the creature that serveth thee, who art the Maker increaseth his strength against the unrighteous for their punishment, and abateth his strength for the benefit of such as put their trust in thee.

25: Therefore even then was it altered into all fashions, and was obedient to thy grace, that nourisheth all things, according to the desire of them that had need:

26: That thy children, O Lord, whom thou lovest, might know, that it is not the growing of fruits that nourisheth man: but that it is thy word, which preserveth them that put their trust in thee.

27: For that which was not destroyed of the fire, being warmed with a little sunbeam, soon melted away:

28: That it might be known, that we must prevent the sun to give thee thanks, and at the dayspring pray unto thee.

29: For the hope of the unthankful shall melt away as the winter's hoar frost, and shall run away as unprofitable water.

Chapter Seventeen

1: For great are thy judgments, and cannot be expressed: therefore unnurtured souls have erred.

2: For when unrighteous men thought to oppress the holy nation; they being shut up in their houses, the prisoners of darkness, and fettered with the bonds of a long night, lay [there] exiled from the eternal providence.

3: For while they supposed to lie hid in their secret sins, they were scattered under a dark veil of forgetfulness, being horribly astonished, and troubled with [strange] apparitions.

4: For neither might the corner that held them keep them from fear: but noises [as of waters] falling down sounded about them, and sad visions appeared unto them with heavy countenances.

5: No power of the fire might give them light: neither could the bright flames of the stars endure to lighten that horrible night.

6: Only there appeared unto them a fire kindled of itself, very dreadful: for being much terrified, they thought the things which they saw to be worse than the sight they saw not.

7: As for the illusions of art magick, they were put down, and their vaunting in wisdom was reproved with disgrace.

8: For they, that promised to drive away terrors and troubles from a sick soul, were sick themselves of fear, worthy to be laughed at.

9: For though no terrible thing did fear them; yet being scared with beasts that passed by, and hissing of serpents,

10: They died for fear, denying that they saw the air, which could of no side be avoided.

11: For wickedness, condemned by her own witness, is very timorous, and being pressed with conscience, always forecasteth grievous things.

12: For fear is nothing else but a betraying of the succours which reason offereth.

13: And the expectation from within, being less, counteth the ignorance more than the cause which bringeth the torment.

14: But they sleeping the same sleep that night, which was indeed intolerable, and which came upon them out of the bottoms of inevitable hell,

15: Were partly vexed with monstrous apparitions, and partly fainted, their heart failing them: for a sudden fear, and not looked for, came upon them.

16: So then whosoever there fell down was straitly kept, shut up in a prison without iron bars,

17: For whether he were husbandman, or shepherd, or a labourer in the field, he was overtaken, and endured that necessity, which could not be avoided: for they were all bound with one chain of darkness.

18: Whether it were a whistling wind, or a melodious noise of birds among the spreading branches, or a pleasing fall of water running violently,

19: Or a terrible sound of stones cast down, or a running that could not be seen of skipping beasts, or a roaring voice of most savage wild beasts, or a rebounding echo from the hollow mountains; these things made them to swoon for fear.
20: For the whole world shined with clear light, and none were hindered in their labour:

21: Over them only was spread an heavy night, an image of that darkness which should afterward receive them: but yet were they unto themselves more grievous than the darkness.

Chapter Eighteen

1: Nevertheless thy saints had a very great light, whose voice they hearing, and not seeing their shape, because they also had not suffered the same things, they counted them happy.

2: But for that they did not hurt them now, of whom they had been wronged before, they thanked them, and besought them pardon for that they had been enemies.

3: Instead whereof thou gavest them a burning pillar

of fire, both to be a guide of the unknown journey, and an harmless sun to entertain them honourably.
4: For they were worthy to be deprived of light and imprisoned in darkness, who had kept thy sons shut up, by whom the uncorrupt light of the law was to be given unto the world.

5: And when they had determined to slay the babes of the saints, one child being cast forth, and saved, to reprove them, thou tookest away the multitude of their children, and destroyedst them altogether in a mighty water.
6: Of that night were our fathers certified afore, that assuredly knowing unto what oaths they had given credence, they might afterwards be of good cheer.

7: So of thy people was accepted both the salvation of the righteous, and destruction of the enemies.

8: For wherewith thou didst punish our adversaries, by the same thou didst glorify us, whom thou hadst called.

9: For the righteous children of good men did sacrifice secretly, and with one consent made a holy law, that the saints should be like partakers of the same good and evil, the fathers now singing out the songs of praise.

10: But on the other side there sounded an ill according cry of the enemies, and a lamentable noise was carried abroad for children that were bewailed.

11: The master and the servant were punished after one manner; and like as the king, so suffered the common person.

12: So they all together had innumerable dead with one kind of death; neither were the living sufficient to bury them: for in one moment the noblest offspring of them was destroyed.

13: For whereas they would not believe any thing by reason of the enchantments; upon the destruction of the firstborn, they acknowledged this people to be the sons of God.

14: For while all things were in quiet silence, and that night was in the midst of her swift course,

15: Thine Almighty word leaped down from heaven out of thy royal throne, as a fierce man of war into the midst of a land of destruction,

16: And brought thine unfeigned commandment as a sharp sword, and standing up filled all things with death; and it touched the heaven, but it stood upon the earth.

17: Then suddenly visions of horrible dreams troubled them sore, and terrors came upon them unlooked for.

18: And one thrown here, and another there, half dead, shewed the cause of his death.

19: For the dreams that troubled them did foreshew this, lest they should perish, and not know why they were afflicted.

20: Yea, the tasting of death touched the righteous also, and there was a destruction of the multitude in the wilderness: but the wrath endured not long.

21: For then the blameless man made haste, and stood forth to defend them; and bringing the shield of his proper ministry, even prayer, and the propitiation of incense, set himself against the wrath, and so brought the calamity to an end, declaring that he was thy servant.

22: So he overcame the destroyer, not with strength of body, nor force of arms, but with a word subdued him that punished, alleging the oaths and covenants made with the fathers.

23: For when the dead were now fallen down by heaps one upon another, standing between, he stayed the wrath, and parted the way to the living.

24: For in the long garment was the whole world, and in the four rows of the stones was the glory of the fathers graven, and thy Majesty upon the daidem of his head.

25: Unto these the destroyer gave place, and was afraid of them: for it was enough that they only tasted of the wrath.

Chapter Nineteen

1: As for the ungodly, wrath came upon them without mercy unto the end: for he knew before what they would do;

2: How that having given them leave to depart, and sent them hastily away, they would repent and pursue them.

3: For whilst they were yet mourning and making

lamentation at the graves of the dead, they added another foolish device, and pursued them as fugitives, whom they had intreated to be gone.

4: For the destiny, whereof they were worthy, drew them unto this end, and made them forget the things that had already happened, that they might fulfill the punishment which was wanting to their torments:

5: And that thy people might pass a wonderful way: but they might find a strange death.

6: For the whole creature in his proper kind was fashioned again anew, serving the peculiar commandments that were given unto them, that thy children might be kept without hurt:

7: As namely, a cloud shadowing the camp; and where water stood before, dry land appeared; and out of the Red sea a way without impediment; and out of the violent stream a green field:

8: Wherethrough all the people went that were defended with thy hand, seeing thy marvellous strange wonders.

9: For they went at large like horses, and leaped like lambs, praising thee, O Lord, who hadst delivered them.

10: For they were yet mindful of the things that were done while they sojourned in the strange land, how the ground brought forth flies instead of cattle, and how the river cast up a multitude of frogs instead of fishes.

11: But afterwards they saw a new generation of fowls, when, being led with their appetite, they asked delicate meats.

12: For quails came up unto them from the sea for their contentment.

13: And punishments came upon the sinners not without former signs by the force of thunders: for they suffered justly according to their own wickedness, insomuch as they used a more hard and hateful behaviour toward strangers.

14: For the Sodomites did not receive those, whom they knew not when they came: but these brought friends into bondage, that had well deserved of them.

15: And not only so, but peradventure some respect shall be had of those, because they used strangers not friendly:

16: But these very grievously afflicted them, whom

they had received with feastings, and were already made partakers of the same laws with them.

17: Therefore even with blindness were these stricken, as those were at the doors of the righteous man: when, being compassed about with horrible great darkness, every one sought the passage of his own doors.

18: For the elements were changed in themselves by a kind of harmony, like as in a psaltery notes change the name of the tune, and yet are always sounds; which may well be perceived by the sight of the things that have been done.

19: For earthly things were turned into watery, and the things, that before swam in the water, now went upon the ground.

20: The fire had power in the water, forgetting his own virtue: and the water forgat his own quenching nature.

21: On the other side, the flames wasted not the flesh of the corruptible living things, though they walked therein; neither melted they the icy kind of heavenly meat that was of nature apt to melt.

22: For in all things, O Lord, thou didst magnify thy

people, and glorify them, neither didst thou lightly regard them: but didst assist them in every time and place.

End

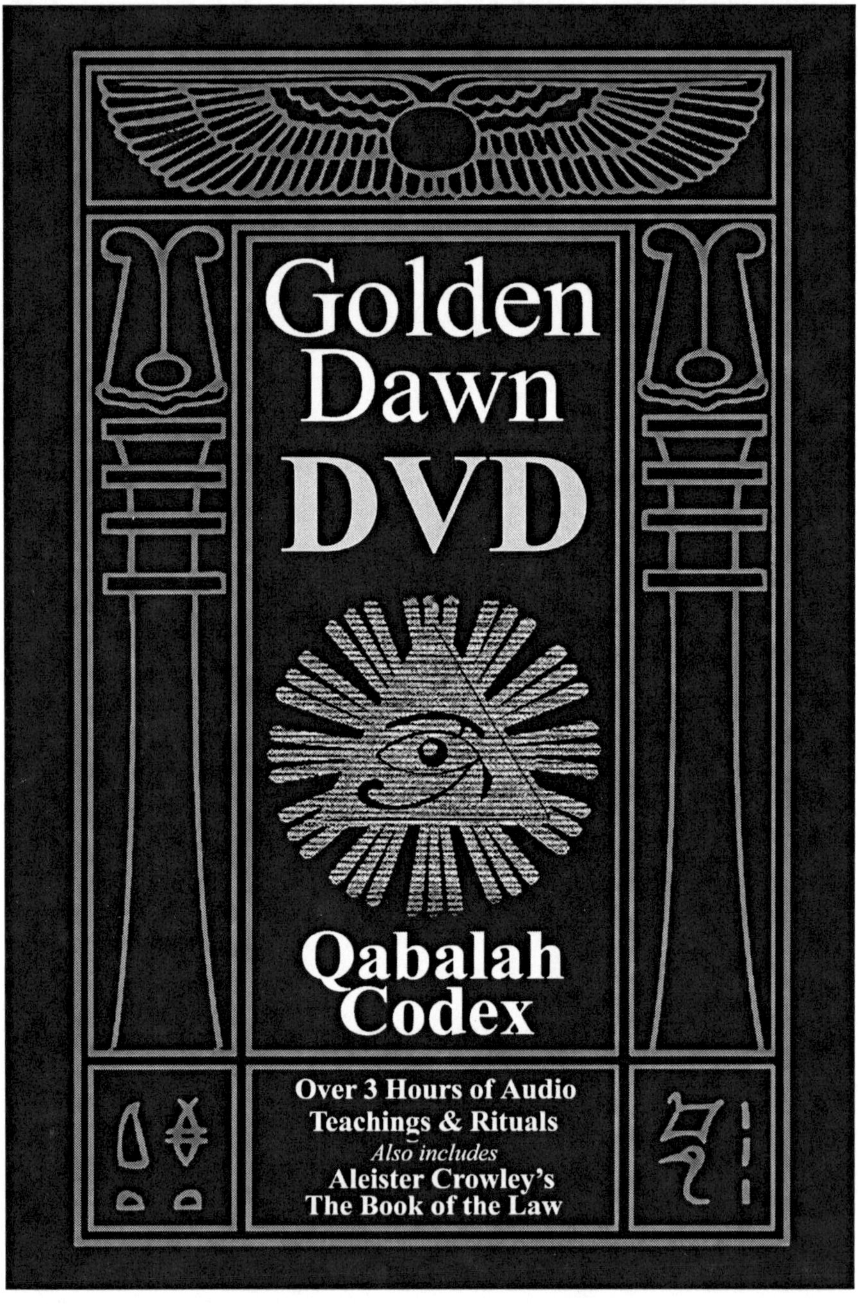
Golden
Dawn
DVD
Qabalah
Codex
Over 3 Hours of Audio
Teachings & Rituals
Also includes
Aleister Crowley's
The Book of the Law

THE GOLDEN DAWN QABALAH CODEX DVD

The Collected Qabalah Audio teachings of Steven Ashe

Contents:

The Qabalah and the Magical Tradition, The philosophy of Magick and Mysticism, Self Development and Occult practices, Initiation and the Qabalah, The Sephiroth Belimah - Voices from Nothing , Macrocosm and Microcosm Gemetria & the sacred alphabet, The Angels of the Schemhamphorash , History of the Literary Qabalah, The Sephiroth upon the Tree of Life, Malkuth and Daath: The Fall, The Four worlds of the Qabalist, The Rite of the Pentagram , The Qabalah of 50 Gates , The Three orders of Being, Psycho-Static; Psycho-Kinetic; Psycho-Telios

Aleister Crowley's The Book of the Law (full length audio)

Methods of Invocation
The Binding of the Qlipoth
The Grand Qabalistic Invocation
Consecration the Water, Salt & Ash
The Seven Great Planetary Invocations
7 Lectures on Advanced Qabalah
& the experience of the Astral Sephiroth

Plus 6 Full length e-Books
Complete Rituals of the Golden Dawn (355pages)
The Enochian Magic of the Golden Dawn (105 pages)
The Qabalah Codex (188 Pages - including the text of the ritual invocations above)
The Hermetic Qabalah of Anna Kingsford
The Key of Solomon (including seals & talismans)
The Book of Enoch (The Book of the Watchers) - 1st Century BC text of Qabalah tradition dealing with the lore of the fallen angels.

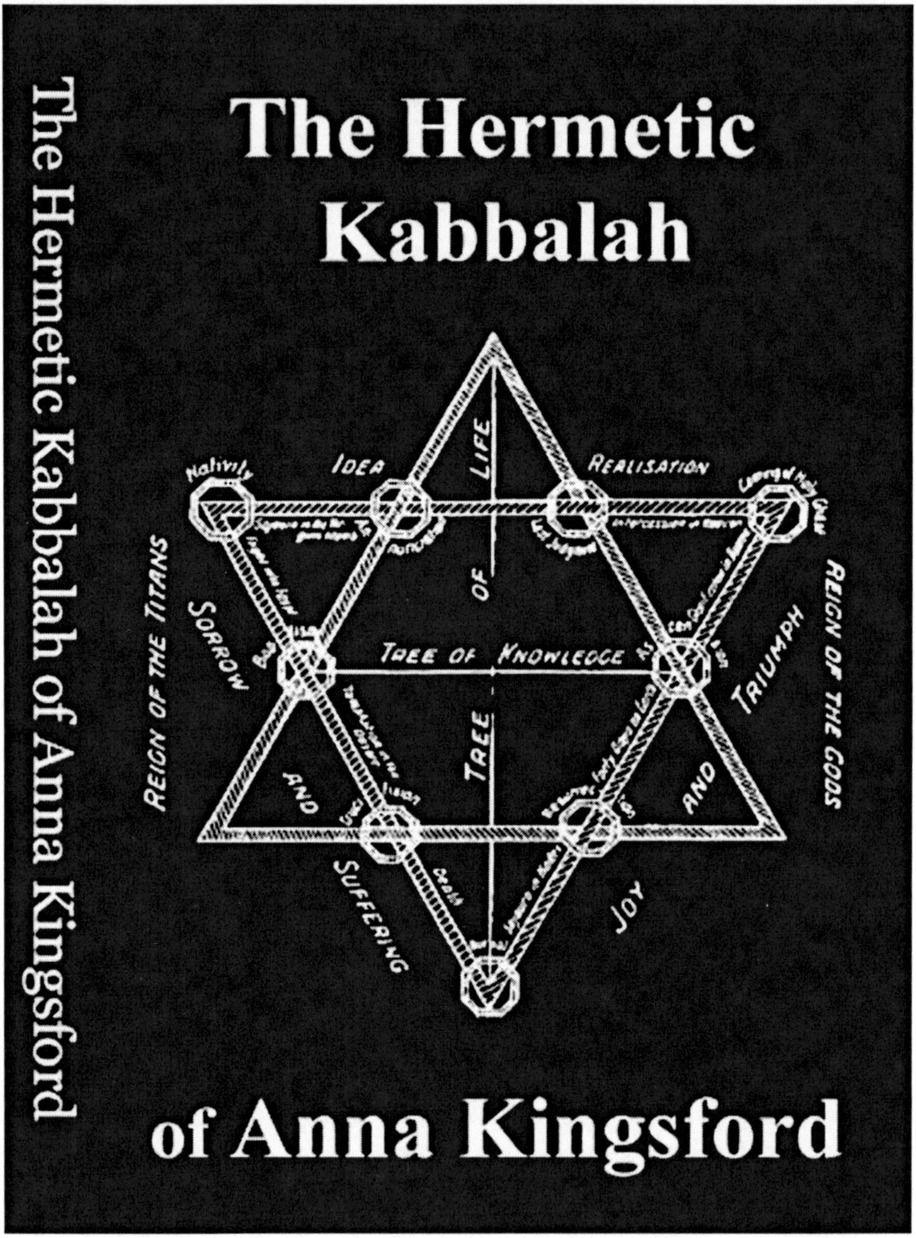
The Hermetic Kabbalah of Anna Kingsford
The Hermetic Kabbalah
Nativity
IDEA
LIFE
REALISATION
REIGN OF THE TITANS
SORROW
OF
TREE OF KNOWLEDGE
TRIUMPH
REIGN OF THE GODS
TREE
AND
AND
SUFFERING
JOY
of Anna Kingsford

The Hermetic Kabbalah of Anna Kingsford

The Hermetic Kabbalah of Anna Kingsford, The Credo of Christendom & other addresses and essays on Esoteric Christianity, by Anna Kingsford and Edward Maitland represented for the 21st century enquirer. In 1883 Anna Kingsford was made President of the Theosophical Society, promoted a Western, Christian and Hermetic Esotericism. She claimed to recieve mystical insights in trance states and sleep, she was an advocate of women's rights anti-vivisection & vegetarianism. Mahatma Gandhi is said to have sold her books.

The Hermetic Kabbalah of Anna Kingsford

ISBN: 978-1-84753-313-5

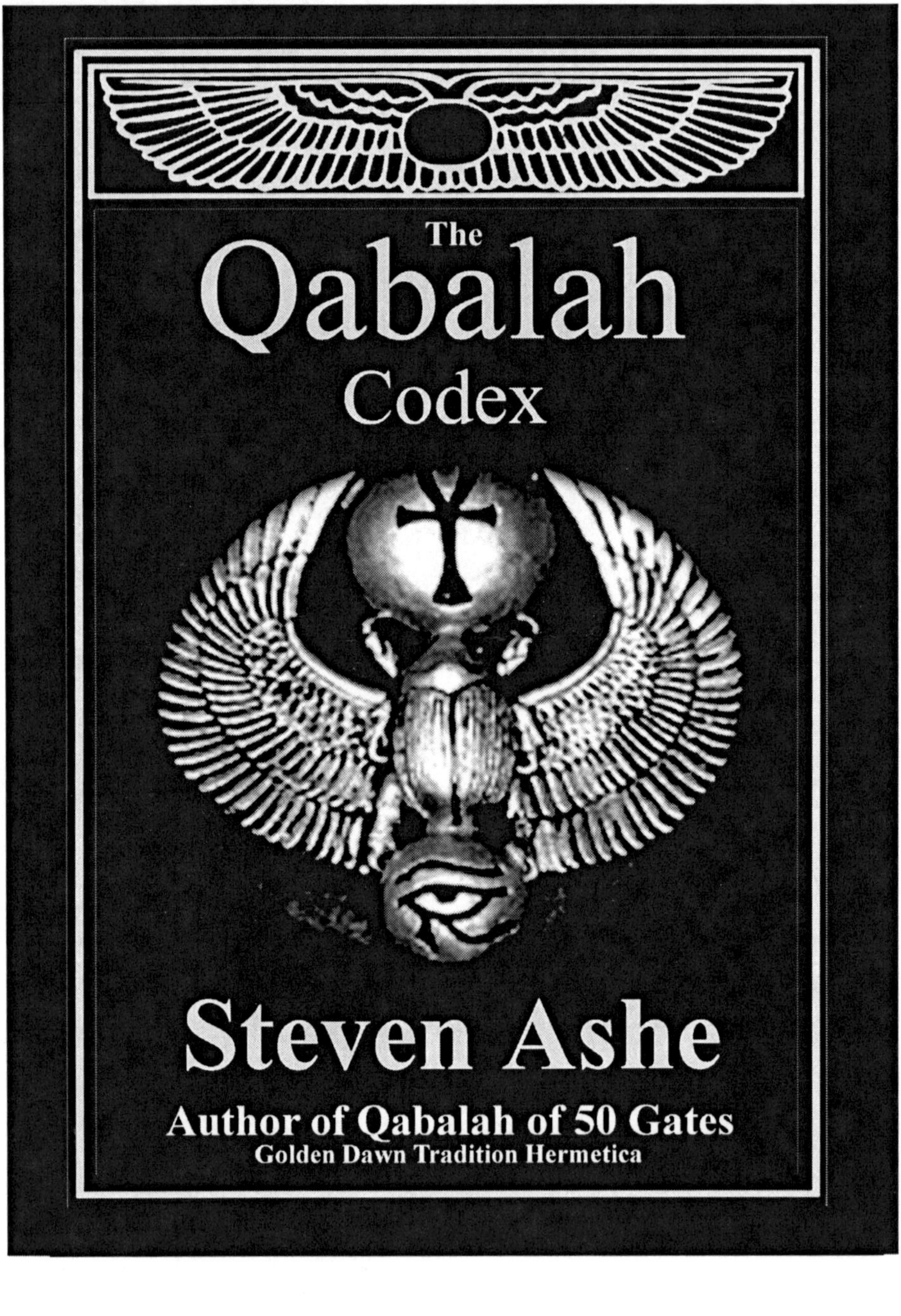
The
Qabalah
Codex
Steven Ashe
Author of Qabalah of 50 Gates
Golden Dawn Tradition Hermetica

The Qabalah Codex

by Steven Ashe

Containing teachings on the fundamentals of Qabalistic theory, an initiated commentary upon the Tarot and Qabalistic symbolism, the official planetary & zodiacal invocations of the Golden Dawn lodge of the FSR, Zodiacal Magic, the planetary and zodiacal significance of the 72 Angels of the Shemhamphorash (Divided Name), essential esoteric rites for the Opening of the Temple, the Sidereal Zodiac and the employment of the Angels with relevance to the fixed-stars, etc. From the author of *Qabalah of 50 Gates* and *The Complete Golden Dawn Initiate.*

The Qabalah Codex

ISBN: **978-1-84753-730-0**

Printed in the United Kingdom
by Lightning Source UK Ltd.
130289UK00001B/249/P

9 780955 693229